Book of Satanic Ritual

The Companion to *Book of Satanic Magic*

Aleister Nacht

Book of Satanic Ritual

© 2012 Aleister Nacht

Published by
Loki / Speckbohne Publishing
All rights reserved

No part of this book may be reproduced by any means without prior written permission of the publisher.

First Edition

10 9 8 7 6 5 4 3 2 1

Book of Satanic Ritual

We are the Saints of Hell....

Book of Satanic Ritual

ABYSS
LORD OF CHAOS

Book of Satanic Ritual

Table of Contents

Part I	Page 7
Part II	Page 35
Part III	Page 91
Part IV	Page 147

Book of Satanic Ritual

♐

ADNACHIEL
THE HUNTER DEMON

Book of Satanic Ritual

ANAEL
DEMON OF LUST

PART I

The book you now hold in your hand is the product of Satanic inspiration. While writing this work, I asked Satan and His Demons to bless the words and provide a vision for me, *a humble servant of the most High Lord Satan*, to follow and reveal as He desired. Satan answered my prayer and showed me what He desired for you, the reader, to know and understand. It is with this knowledge I solemnly submit this work and dedicate it to Satan.

This manuscript has been Satanically blessed through countless rituals and dedications in the presence of several different covens. With the spilling of blood, urine, sweat, semen and tears this work has received energy and power from a

Book of Satanic Ritual

host of demons. These magical creatures actually held the manuscript and interceded to Lord Satan on our behalf; **TO SATAN BE THE GLORY!**

In the early and late hours of countless rituals and masses, these words have slowly been released into the air as energy and returned herein as the truth. So laborious and yet so succinct, pure evil has been poured into these passages in such a way as to release the energy upon being read aloud by YOU, the reader.

As candles burned and incense filled every corner of the inner sanctums, these letters and characters are alive with purpose and a magnetism of epic proportion. The altar has spread her beautiful legs to receive us all who call Satan "Master". She has screamed with grim delight as the darkness opened and Hell entered the sanctum to praise the most high. She has kissed the pages and her fluids have been used to draw the *Sigil of Satan* upon the manuscript.

We have chanted and invited the Hosts of Hell to partake of our ceremonies. Pleasure to pain, hate to love and physical to spiritual we have dedicated each and every page you hold in you hands.

The power of Satan; that is what you are now

holding and it is alive with every breath you take. They will come if you call and your magic will be heightened if you believe.

These forces are real and you must proceed with respect and caution for you hold a sword with two edges. One will again rip through the shroud of the sanctum while the other will destroy you if you act foolishly. Black magic is a balance of belief and respect. If you wish to anger Satan to provoke a response, you may very well do so with this book. Satan has no mercy and He will take all He desires from you. I have warned those terminally stupid and watched their skin fall from the bones. If you test the Master of the World you will receive His wrath fully.

Black Angels surround us all just one dimension removed. From the top of the pinnacle to the bottom of the grave, these beings receive their charge from Satan, Lucifer, Belial and Leviathan. They are about the Father's work.

You will view life differently after submitting your soul to the desires of Satan. This book will point a way for your journey. Trample the books of the liars under your feet and invite the KING of the coming trials. Serve Him and He will serve you

Book of Satanic Ritual

well.

Time is upon you and the invitation will never be as accessible to you as at this moment. The curtain opens to reveal the coming of OUR TIME.....yes it is upon us now!! Your place is waiting in the King's court. Satan is waiting and if you accept and believe, you will have nothing to fear ever again.

The bell is sounding...........**Hail Satan!!**

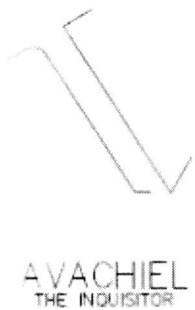

AVACHIEL
THE INQUISITOR

Hell

Hell appears in several mythologies and religions. It is commonly inhabited by demons and the souls of dead people. A fable about hell which recurs in folklore across several cultures is the allegory of the long spoons. Hell is often depicted in art and literature, perhaps most famously in Dante's Divine Comedy.

In his Divina commedia ("Divine comedy"; set in the year 1300), Dante Alighieri employed the concept of taking Virgil as his guide through Inferno (and then, in the second canticle, up the mountain of Purgatorio). Virgil himself is not condemned to Hell in Dante's poem but is rather, as a virtuous pagan, confined to Limbo just at the edge of Hell. The geography of Hell is very elaborately laid out in this work, with nine concentric rings leading deeper into the Earth and deeper into the various punishments of Hell, until, at the center of the world, Dante finds Satan himself trapped in the frozen lake of Cocytus. A small tunnel leads past Satan and out to the other side of the world, at the base of the Mount of Purgatory.

John Milton's Paradise Lost (1667) opens with the fallen angels, including their leader Satan, waking up in Hell after having been defeated in the war in heaven and the action returns there at several points throughout the poem. Milton portrays Hell as the abode of the demons, and the passive prison from which they plot their revenge upon Heaven through the corruption of the human race. 19th century French poet Arthur Rimbaud alluded to the concept as well in the title and themes of one of his major works, A Season In

Hell. Rimbaud's poetry portrays his own suffering in a poetic form as well as other themes.

Many of the great epics of European literature include episodes that occur in Hell. In the Roman poet Virgil's Latin epic, the Aeneid, Aeneas descends into Dis (the underworld) to visit his father's spirit. The underworld is only vaguely described, with one unexplored path leading to the punishments of Tartarus, while the other leads through Erebus and the Elysian Fields.

The idea of Hell was highly influential to writers such as Jean-Paul Sartre who authored the 1944 play "No Exit" about the idea that "Hell is other people". Although not a religious man, Sartre was fascinated by his interpretation of a Hellish state of suffering. C.S. Lewis's The Great Divorce (1945) borrows its title from William Blake's Marriage of Heaven and Hell (1793) and its inspiration from the Divine Comedy as the narrator is likewise guided through Hell and Heaven. Hell is portrayed here as an endless, desolate twilight city upon which night is imperceptibly sinking. The night is actually the Apocalypse, and it heralds the arrival of the demons after their judgment. Before the night comes, anyone can escape Hell if they leave behind their former selves and accept Heaven's offer, and a journey to Heaven reveals that Hell is infinitely small; it is nothing more or less than what happens to a soul that turns away from God and into itself.

Hell by other names includes:

Abaddon

The Hebrew word Abaddon, meaning "destruction", is sometimes used as a synonym of Hell.[46]

Gehenna

In the New Testament, both early (i.e. the KJV) and modern translations often translate Gehenna as "Hell."[47] Young's Literal Translation is one notable exception, simply using "Gehenna", which was in fact a geographic location just outside Jerusalem (the Valley of Hinnom).

Hades

Hades is the Greek word traditionally used for the

Hebrew word Sheol in such works as the Septuagint, the Greek translations of the Hebrew Bible. Like other first-century Jews literate in Greek, Christian writers of the New Testament followed this use. While earlier translations most often translated Hades as "hell", as does the King James Version, modern translations use the transliteration "Hades",[48] or render the word as allusions "to the grave",[49] "among the dead",[50] "place of the dead"[51] and many other like statements in other verses. In Latin, Hades could be translated as Purgatorium (Purgatory in English use) after about 1200 A.D.,[52] but no modern English translations Hades to Purgatory. See Intermediate state.

Infernus
The Latin word infernus means "being underneath" and is often translated as "Hell".

Sheol
In the King James Bible, the Old Testament term Sheol is translated as "Hell" 31 times.[53] However, Sheol was translated as "the grave" 31

other times.[54] Sheol is also translated as "the pit" three times.[55]

Modern translations, however, do not translate Sheol as "Hell" at all, instead rendering it "the grave," "the pit," or "death." See Intermediate state.

Tartarus

Appearing only in II Peter 2:4 in the New Testament, both early and modern translations often translate Tartarus as "Hell." Again, Young's Literal Translation is an exception, using "Tartarus".

Book of Satanic Ritual

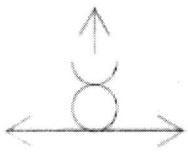

BARBIEL
LORD OF ANCIENTS

From a logical aspect, ritual is nothing more than a well choreographed dance or play. To the Satanist, it is much more and deeper in meaning. Every word, letter and sign has a distinct meaning and all elements play a part in the greater whole. To shortcut any of the steps would be to risk failure of the desired result......a waste of time for the practitioner. In thought or other perceived observation, the ritual is created in the mind long before being brought to fruition as reality.

The essence of Satanic ritual, and Satanism itself, if taken out of logic rather than desperation, is to objectively enter into a subjective state. It must be realized, however, that human behavior is almost totally motivated by subjective impulse.

It is difficult therefore, to try to be objective once

Book of Satanic Ritual

the emotions have established their preferences. Since man is the only animal who can lie to himself and believe it, he must consciously strive for some degree of self-awareness. Inasmuch as ritual magic is dependent upon emotional intensity for success, all manner of emotion producing devices must be employed in its practice.

An altar, for instance, can add dramatic effect to the ritual. A beautiful Satanic beauty with legs spread widely would be enough for some to enter a heightened state of awareness. To touch her, smell her and taste her would truly rock the foundations of the altar table. Spells and magic are intensified with stimulation and in ritual, all present should be at their height of stimulation.

The basic ingredients in the casting of a spell can be categorized as desire, timing, imagery, direction, and balance. The material contained in this volume represents the type of Satanic rite, which has been employed in the past for *specialized* productive or destructive ends.

Because ritual so often exerts such change, both within the chamber and as an aftermath in the outside world, it is easy to assume that the Lord's

Book of Satanic Ritual

Prayer recited backwards is usually linked with the *Black Mass* and is also synonymous with Satanism. In my opinion, there are a few necessary things a Satanist must have in order for magical workings to fully succeed. The most important is the sense of conclusion. The practitioner must have a vivid idea of what he / she desires from the ritual. To begin a ritual without knowing what is expected will always end badly. All the planning and preparation in the world will not compensate for a clear expectation. How can you arrive at the right place if you do not select a destination before beginning a journey?

Ritual is no different. Select the results you desire long before the ritual begins. Failure to do this is by nature, stupid and stupidity is not a flattering attribute for a Satanist.

If you do not have a dedicated sanctum, do not worry. There are many fantastic locations for rituals probably (and literally) in your backyard. Pesky neighbors not withstanding, a secluded backyard is the perfect place to perform Satanic

Book of Satanic Ritual

rituals. You will be in a secure place and can control access to those you wish to attend. If needed, you an ask the police to remove any trespassers as you wish.

I have always loved rituals under the open sky and if you have access to such an area, I highly recommend it. I must admit, blood does look quite black in the moonlight.

I do not recommend public parks or other public areas. Observers will only detract from the energy and will surely cause disruptions as most people mock what they do not understand. Never trespass or violate areas and never break the law including fires where they are prohibited or unsafe. Setting a forest on fire is not only stupid but it is irresponsible.

Evil can manifest anywhere and the physical surroundings are not important. Have been invited to conduct a ritual in the bay of an auto repair shop, which worked really well. Obviously we did not have open flames.

I have also held ceremonies in beautifully

decorated temples of other covens that were lavishly laid out. My coven has one such sanctum that we maintain. It is up to the practitioner.

Satanism indeed represents the opposite viewpoint, and as such acts as a catalyst for change. The fact is, throughout history a "bad guy" has been needed so that those who are "right" can flourish. It was to be expected that the first *Messes Noirs* would institute reversals of existing liturgy, thus reinforcing the original blasphemy of heretical thought.

Modern Satanism realizes man's need for an "other side," and has realistically accepted that polarity-at least within the confines of a ritual chamber. Thus a Satanic chamber can serve - depending upon the degree of embellishment and the extent of the acts within - as a meditation chamber for the entertainment of unspoken thoughts, or a veritable palace of perversity. That is totally up to the practitioner.

Rituals dealing with the invocation of spirits of the dead and resurrection of corpses as well as magical seals, charms, and spells have been omitted from this book in order to avoid such things being used foolishly by those who have no interest in magic beyond the acquisition of wealth and the satisfaction of vain ambitions. If you desire it the spirits will reveal to you all manner of sorceries whereby you may attain that which you desire. This book provides the key to crossing the Gates of Hell and becoming one with the Forces of Darkness. Rather than give you spells, charms, and seals for material benefit, this book provides you with the means to acquire these things yourself.

Initial to performing these rituals, you must take a "Bath of Purification", a bath in salt water. The reason for this is that salt is a universal purging agent. Taking a bath in salt water will remove any psychic influence, either "positive" or "negative". This will remove any curse or blessing and temporarily eliminate the presence of any spirit or demon. Fill your bath with hot water, throw a cup of rock salt into the bath, and then enter into the water. You must submerge your entire body in the water to ensure that all psychic influence is removed from you. Once done, you will be in a "neutral" starting position from which to begin these rites. It is important that you only do this once, preliminary to performing these rites. If you take another "Bath of Purification" later you will have to start the rituals over again.

The rituals can take any form you choose. It is not essential to shut out all outside light sources unless you are prone to distraction. You may adapt the rituals to your liking but they must be committed to memory. For this reason, I have left the invocations simple and repetitive. You will have no problem memorizing the invocations and can easily add your own embellishments when you enter the ritual chamber.

In the performance of these rites you shall set yourself apart to the Forces of Darkness, consecrate your body as a temple to the Dark Lord, cross the Gates of Hell, and become one with the Forces of Darkness. This differs from all other systems of magic involving the invocation of spirits. White magicians stand inside protective pentagrams wearing protective amulets to shield themselves from the forces they call upon.

In the Satanic Bible, Anton LaVey mocked the hypocrisy of those who attempted to protect themselves from the forces they called upon for aid. Satanic priests have known for many years that the "Forces of Darkness" could be invoked (or more correctly "evoked") into the sorcerer's body, but rituals of this type have never been made available to the aspiring witch or wizard because of the inherent danger in such rituals. In other rituals demons are invoked as external forces (friendly, perhaps, but external to the magician) which may be directed and controlled by the Satanist. Many less-experienced practitioners still fear these forces which they call upon as something alien to themselves and "evil".

What will become apparent to the practitioner of these rites is that Satan, Lucifer, Belial, and Leviathan are aspects of the human psyche, archetypes which exist within the subconscious and sub rational mind, not external beings which can in any way influence the magician to good or evil ends. The objective of this system of magic is not to "invoke" Satan to physical appearance (for that would be mere hallucination) but rather to become Satan (or to actualize that aspect of the psyche which is called "Satan"); not to "invoke" Lucifer but to become Lucifer; not to "invoke" Belial but to become Belial; not to "invoke" Leviathan but to become Leviathan. The purpose of these invocations is to achieve power,

Book of Satanic Ritual

knowledge, and enlightenment by activating those parts of the brain which have been called the "Forces of Darkness".

Renunciation & Proclamation (recite three times)
I renounce God.
I renounce Jesus.
I renounce the angels and archangels.
I renounce the Holy Catholic Church.
I renounce all that is holy and all that is good.
I renounce all gods.
And I proclaim that Satan Lucifer is Lord of this World.
I proclaim that Satan Lucifer is God of the Earth.
I proclaim that Satan Lucifer is my Master.
(drink from chalice)

Pact Giving Body, Mind, & Soul (write upon parchment, recite three times, then burn.)
I give my body to Lucifer.
I give my mind to Lucifer.
I give my soul to Lucifer.
My flesh is His Flesh.
My blood is His Blood.

(drink from chalice then......)
Lucifer accept this, my sacrifice.

Consecration of Body in the name of Satan and Lucifer

I bless and consecrate these feet in the name of Satan and in the name of Lucifer. (repeat three times).

I bless and consecrate these legs in the name of Satan and in the name of Lucifer. (repeat three times).

I bless and consecrate these genitals in the name of Satan and in the name of Lucifer. (repeat three times).

I bless and consecrate this penis in the name of Satan and in the name of Lucifer. (repeat three times).

I bless and consecrate this abdomen in the name of Satan and in the name of Lucifer. (repeat three times).

I bless and consecrate this chest in the name of Satan and in the name of Lucifer. (repeat three times).

I bless and consecrate these buttocks in the name of Satan and in the name of Lucifer. (repeat three

times).
I bless and consecrate this back in the name of Satan and in the name of Lucifer. (repeat three times).
I bless and consecrate these hands in the name of Satan and in the name of Lucifer. (repeat three times).
I bless and consecrate these arms in the name of Satan and in the name of Lucifer. (repeat three times).
I bless and consecrate these shoulders in the name of Satan and in the name of Lucifer. (repeat three times).
I bless and consecrate this neck in the name of Satan and in the name of Lucifer. (repeat three times).
I bless and consecrate these eyes in the name of Satan and in the name of Lucifer. (repeat three times).
I bless and consecrate this body as a temple to the Dark Lord. (repeat three times).
I bless and consecrate this temple in the name of Satan and in the name of Lucifer. (repeat three times).
I set myself apart to the Dark Lord and to the

Forces of Darkness. (repeat three times).
I bless and consecrate this body in the name of Satan and in the name of Lucifer. (repeat three times).
(drink from chalice)

Invocation of the Unholy Trinity
Unholy Trinity of Hell, I invoke thee.
Unholy Trinity of Hell, I summon thee.
Unholy Trinity of Hell, I conjure thee.
Come forth, Unholy Trinity of Hell, and manifest thyself
Within this body, this temple which I have prepared.
Come forth, Unholy Trinity of Hell, and manifest thyself.
Fill me with the Unholy Spirit.
Come forth, Unholy Trinity of Hell, and manifest thyself.
(drink from chalice)

Invocation of the Unholy Spirit
Unholy Spirit, I invoke thee.
Unholy Spirit, I summon thee.

Unholy Spirit, I conjure thee.
Come forth, Unholy Spirit, and manifest thyself
Within this body, this temple which I have prepared.
Come forth, Unholy Spirit, and manifest thyself.
Come forth, Unholy Spirit, and manifest thyself.
(drink from chalice)

Invocation of the Nine Lords of the Abyss
The Nine Great Lords of the Abyss, I invoke thee.
The Nine Great Lords of the Abyss, I summon thee.
The Nine Great Lords of the Abyss, I conjure thee.
Come forth, Nine Great Lords of the Abyss, and manifest thyselves
Within this body, this temple which I have prepared.
Come forth, Nine Great Lords of the Abyss, and manifest thyselves.
Send unto me my Unholy Guardian Demon,
And come forth, Nine Great Lords of the Abyss, and manifest thyselves.
(drink from chalice)

Book of Satanic Ritual

Invocation of Your Unholy Guardian Demon

My Unholy Guardian Demon, I invoke thee.
My Unholy Guardian Demon, I summon thee.
My Unholy Guardian Demon, I conjure thee.
Come forth, my Unholy Guardian Demon, and manifest thyself
Within this body, this temple which I have prepared.
Come forth, my Unholy Guardian Demon, and manifest thyself.
Come forth, my Unholy Guardian Demon, and manifest thyself.
(drink from chalice)

Invocation of Satan

To the south I call, and into the flames of Hell!
Satan, I invoke thee.
Satan, I summon thee.
Satan, I conjure thee.
Come forth, Satan, and manifest thyself
Within this body, within this temple which I have prepared.
Come forth, Satan, and manifest thyself.
Come forth, Satan, and manifest thyself.
Open wide the Gates of Hell that I may cross and

become like you.
Open wide thy Gate that I may cross.
Come forth, Satan, and manifest thyself.
Come forth, Satan, and manifest thyself.
(drink from chalice)

Invocation of Lucifer
To the east I call, and into the air of enlightenment:
Lucifer, I invoke thee.
Lucifer, I summon thee.
Lucifer, I conjure thee.
Come forth, Lucifer, and manifest thyself
Within this body, within this temple which I have prepared.
Come forth, Lucifer, and manifest thyself.
Come forth, Lucifer, and manifest thyself.
Open wide the Gates of Hell that I may cross and become like you.
Open wide thy Gate that I may cross.
Come forth, Lucifer, and manifest thyself.
Come forth, Lucifer, and manifest thyself.
(drink from chalice)

Invocation of Belial
To the north I call, and to the depths of the earth:
Belial, I invoke thee.
Belial, I summon thee.
Belial, I conjure thee.
Come forth, Belial, and manifest thyself
Within this body, within this temple which I have prepared.
Come forth, Belial, and manifest thyself.
Come forth, Belial, and manifest thyself.
Open wide the Gates of Hell that I may cross and become like you.
Open wide thy Gate that I may cross.
Come forth, Belial, and manifest thyself.
Come forth, Belial, and manifest thyself.
(drink from chalice)

Invocation of Leviathan
To the west I call, and to the depths of the sea:
Leviathan, I invoke thee.
Leviathan, I summon thee.
Leviathan, I conjure thee.
Come forth, Leviathan, and manifest thyself
Within this body, within this temple which I have prepared.

Come forth, Leviathan, and manifest thyself.
Come forth, Leviathan, and manifest thyself.
Open wide the Gates of Hell that I may cross and become like you.
Open wide thy Gate that I may cross.
Come forth, Leviathan, and manifest thyself.
Come forth, Leviathan, and manifest thyself.
(drink from chalice)

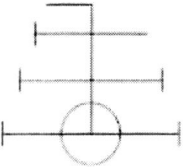

PART II

The Black Mass……."*Messes Noirs*"

Hooded black robes are worn by all participants except two: a woman dressed as a nun, wearing the customary habit and wimple, and the woman who serves as the altar, who is nude.

The one conducting the mass is known as the Celebrant. Over his robe, he wears a necklace bearing the Sigil of Baphomet, the inverted pentagram. Though some versions of the *Black Mass* were performed in vestments consecrated by the Roman Catholic Church, records indicate that such garments were the exception rather than the rule.

The authenticity of a consecrated host seems to have been far more important. The woman who serves as the altar lies on the platform with her body at right angles to its length, her knees at its edge and widely parted. A pillow supports her head. Her arms are outstretched crosswise and each hand grasps a candleholder containing a black candle.

When the celebrant is at the altar, he stands between the altar's knees. Her legs widely spread.

A chalice containing wine or liquor (or whatever is desired) is placed between the altar's thighs. The Ritual Book is placed on a small stand or pillow so that is on the Celebrant's right when he faces the altar. The illuminator stands at the side of the altar near the Ritual Book. Black candles, with one white candle, are used during the ceremony.

Opposite him, on the other side of the altar, stands the thurifer with a thurible that holds ignited charcoal. Next to him stands a participant holding the boat of incense. Music should be liturgical in mood, preferably played on the organ.

Book of Satanic Ritual

The success of magical operations is dependent upon *application of principles learned* rather than the amount of data collected. This rule must be stressed, for ignorance of this fact is the one most consistent cause of magical incompetence and the least likely to be considered as the reason for failure.

Participants:
Altar Priest - lies naked upon altar
Priestess - in white robes
Mistress of Earth - in scarlet robes
Master (Celebrant) - in purple robe
Sub deacon and Illuminator - in black robes
Congregation - in black robes

Setting:
Usually an indoor Temple. If outdoors, clearings in forests or woods are suitable. Caves are ideal. The reason for such Outdoor settings are to provide an impression of 'enclosure'.

Versions:
The Black Mass exists in several versions. The one given below is the version most often used today

but other versions are also included.

Although the *Black Mass* is a ritual that has been performed countless times, the participants often were not Satanists, but would act solely on the idea that <u>*anything*</u> contradictory to the church must be good. During the Inquisition, anyone who doubted the sovereignty of God, Christ and the church was summarily considered a servant of Satan and suffered accordingly.

When all are assembled in the inner sanctum, the bell is sounded nine times and the celebrant, with the Sub deacon and Illuminator preceding him, enters and approaches the altar.

They halt somewhat short of the altar, the Sub deacon placing himself at the Celebrant's left, the Illuminator at his right. The three make a profound bow before the altar and commence the ritual with the following verses and responses.

Book of Satanic Ritual

The Ceremony Begins

The Mistress of Earth turns to the congregation, makes the sign of the inverted pentagram with her left hand, saying:

I will go down to the altars in Hell.

The Priestess responds by saying:

To Satan, the giver of life.

All:
Our Father which wert in heaven hallowed be thy name In heaven as it is on Earth. Give us this day our ecstasy And deliver us to evil as well as temptation For we are your kingdom for aeons and aeons.

Celebrant:
In nomine Magni Dei Nostri Satanas. Introibo ad altare Domini Inferi.

The four cardinal directions of the compass are invoked with the sword.
May Satan the all-powerful Prince of Darkness

And Lord of Earth Grant us our desires.

All:
Prince of Darkness, hear us!
I believe in one Prince, Satan, who reigns over this Earth,
And in one Law which triumphs over all. I believe in one Temple
Our Temple to Satan, and in one Word which triumphs over all:
The Word of ecstasy. And I believe in the Law of the Aeon,
Which is sacrifice, and in the letting of blood
For which I shed no tears since I give praise to my Prince
The fire-giver and look forward to his reign
And the pleasures that are to come!
The Mistress kisses the Master, then turns to the congregation, saying:

May Satan be with you.

Sub deacon and Illuminator:
Ad eum qui laefificat meum.

Book of Satanic Ritual

Adjutorium nostrum in nomine Domini Inferi.
Qui regit terram.

Celebrant:
Before the mighty and ineffable Prince of Darkness, and in the presence of all the dread demons of the Pit, and this assembled company, I acknowledge and confess my past error. Renouncing all past allegiances, I proclaim that Satan-Lucifer rules the earth, and I ratify and renew my promise to recognize and honor Him in all things, without reservation, desiring in return His manifold assistance in the successful completion of my endeavors and the fulfillment of my desires. I call upon you, my Brother, to bear witness and to do likewise.

Sub deacon and Illuminator:
Before the mighty and ineffable Prince of Darkness, and in the presence of all the dread demons of the Pit, and this assembled company, we acknowledge and confess our past error. Renouncing all past allegiances, we proclaim that Satan-Lucifer rules the earth, and we ratify and renew our promise to recognize and honor Him

Book of Satanic Ritual

in all things, without reservation, desiring in return His manifold assistance in the successful completion of our endeavors and the fulfillment of our desires. We call upon you, His liegeman and Celebrant, to receive this pledge in His name.

Celebrant:
Gloria Deo, Domino Inferi, et in terra vita hominibus fortibus. Laudamus te, benedicimus te, adoramus te, glorificamus te, gratias agimus tibi propter magnam potentiam tuam: Domine Satanas, Rex Inferus, Imperator omnipotens.

Therefore, O mighty and terrible Lord of Darkness, we entreat You that You receive and accept this sacrifice, which we offer to You on behalf of this assembled company, upon whom You have set Your mark, that You may make us prosper in fullness and length of life, under Thy protection, and may cause to go forth at our bidding Thy dreadful minions, for the fulfillment of our desires and the destruction of our enemies.

Sub deacon and Illuminator:
In concert this night, we ask Thy unfailing

assistance in this particular need. In the unity of unholy fellowship we praise and honor first Thee, Lucifer, Morning Star, and Beelzebub, Lord of Regeneration; then Belial, Prince of the Earth and Angel of Destruction; Leviathan, Beast of Revelation; Abaddon, Angel of the Bottomless Pit; and Asmodeus, Demon of Lust. We call upon the mighty names of Astaroth, Nergal and Behemoth, of Belphegor, Adramelech, and Baalberith, and of all the nameless and formless ones, the mighty and innumerable hosts of Hell, by whose assistance may we be strengthened in mind, body and will.

The celebrant then extends his hands, palms downward, over the altar.

The bell is sounded three times.

Congregation:
Shemhamforash! Ave Satanas!

The Sub deacon brings forth the chamber pot and presents it to the nun, who has come forward. The nun lifts her habit and urinates into the font. As she passes water, the deacon addresses the congregation.

Sub deacon:
She maketh the font resound with the tears of her mortification. The waters of her shame become a shower of blessing in the tabernacle of Satan, for that which hath been withheld pourest forth, and with it, her piety. The great Baphomet, who is in the midst of the throne, shall sustain her, for she is a living fountain of water.

As the nun completes her urination, the Sub deacon continues.

And the Dark Lord shall wipe all tears from her eyes, for He said unto me: It is done! I am Alpha and Omega, the beginning and the end. I will give freely unto him that is athirst of the fountain of the water of life.

The sub deacon removes the font from the nun and holds it before the Celebrant, who dips the aspergeant (a wafer) into the fluid. Then, the Celebrant turns to each of the cardinal compass

Book of Satanic Ritual

points, shaking the aspergeant twice at each point.

Celebrant points with the sword and says:
(facing south) *In the name of Satan, we bless thee with this, the symbol of the rod of life.*

(facing east) *In the name of Satan, we bless thee with this, the symbol of the rod of life.*

(facing north) *In the name of Satan, we bless thee with this, the symbol of the rod of life.*

(facing west) *In the name of Satan, we bless thee with this, the symbol of the rod of life.*

Sub deacon:
Hoc est corpus Jesu Christi.

The Celebrant raises the wafer, placing it between the breasts of the altar, and then touching it to the vaginal area.

The bell is sounded three times.
He replaces the wafer on the paten (a plate) which rests on the altar platform. Taking the chalice into

his hands, he bends low over it, as with the wafer, and whispers the following words.

Celebrant:
To us, Thy faithful children, O Infernal Lord, who glory in our iniquity and trust in your boundless power and might, grant that we may be numbered among Thy chosen. It is ever through you that all gifts come to us; knowledge, power and wealth are yours to bestow.

Renouncing the spiritual paradise of the weak and lowly, we place our trust in Thee, the God of the Flesh, looking to the satisfaction of all our desires, and petitioning all fulfillments in the land of the living.

Sub deacon and Illuminator:
Shemhamforash! Hail Satan!

Celebrant:
Prompted by the precepts of the earth and the inclinations of the flesh, we make bold to say: Our Father which art in Hell, hallowed be Thy name. Thy kingdom is come, Thy will is done; on earth

as it is in Hell! We take this night our rightful due, and trespass not on paths of pain. Lead us unto temptation, and deliver us from false piety, for Thine is the kingdom and the power and the glory forever!

Sub deacon and Illuminator:
And let reason rule the earth.

Celebrant:
Deliver us, O Mighty Satan, from all past error and delusion, that, having set our foot upon the Path of Darkness and vowed ourselves to Thy service, we may not weaken in our resolve, but with Thy assistance, grow in wisdom and strength.

Sub deacon and Illuminator:
Shemhamforash!

The celebrant takes the wafer into his hands, extends it before him, and turns to face the assembled company, saying the following:

Book of Satanic Ritual

Celebrant:
Ecce corpus Jesu Christi, Dominus Humilim et Rex Servorum.

The celebrant raises the wafer to the Baphomet. He continues in great anger.

Celebrant:
Thou, thou whom, in my capacity of Celebrant, I force, whether thou wilt or no, to descend into this host, to incarnate thyself into this bread, artisan of hoaxes, bandit of homage, robber of affection-hear! Since the day when thou didst issue from the complaisant bowels of a false virgin, thou hast failed all thy engagements, belied all thy promises.

Centuries have wept awaiting thee, fugitive god, mute god! Thou wast to redeem man and thou hast not; thou wast to appear in thy glory, and thou steepest. Go, lie, say to the wretch who appeals to thee, "Hope, be patient, suffer; the hospital of souls will receive thee; angels will succour thee; Heaven opens to thee." Imposter! Thou knowest well that the Angels, disgusted at

thy inertness, abandon thee!
Thou wast to be the interpreter of our plaints, the chamberlain of our tears; thou was to convey them to the cosmos and thou hast not done so, for this intercession would disturb thy eternal sleep of happy satiety.

Thy wrath upon him, O Prince of Darkness, and rend him that he may know the extent of Thy anger. Call forth Thy legions that they may witness what we do in Thy name.

Send forth thy messengers to proclaim this deed, and send the Christian minions staggering to their doom. Smite him anew, O Lord of Light, that his angels, cherubim, and seraphim may cower and tremble with fear, prostrating themselves before Thee in respect of Thy power. Send crashing down the gates of Heaven, that the murders of our ancestors may be avenged!

The celebrant inserts the wafer into the vagina of the altar, removes it, holds it aloft to the Baphomet.
The celebrant then dashes it to the floor, where it

Book of Satanic Ritual

is trampled by himself, Sub deacon and Illuminator while the bell is struck continually.

The Celebrant then takes the chalice into his hands, faces the altar, and drinks.

The Celebrant then presents the cup to the altar, who rises to a sitting position and drinks. She reclines after drinking.

Then, the Celebrant presents the cup to each of the members of the assemblage, first to the Sub deacon, followed by the Illuminator, then the others in order of rank and / or seniority in the Order. In administering the cup to each, he uses the following words:

In nomine Magni Dei Nostri Satanas. Hail Satan!

He then bows before the altar and turns to give the blessing of Satan to the assemblage, extending his left hand in the *Cornu* (Sign of the Horns).

All assembled face altar and raise arms in the *Cornu*.

All:
Ave, Satanas!
Hail Satan!

Celebrant:
Let us depart; it is done.

Deacon and Sub deacon:
So it is done. So mote it be.

The Celebrant, Sub deacon and Illuminator bow toward the altar, assist her to a standing position, turn and the four depart the chamber.
The candles are snuffed as everyone leaves the chamber.

As with all ceremonial rituals, it is helpful if all participants know from memory the content and spoken text. It is important that this is done and that the ritual, when undertaken, follows the text on every occasion. The ritual then is more effective as a ritual, enabling the participants to be both more relaxed and more able to enter into the spirit of the rite.

Book of Satanic Ritual

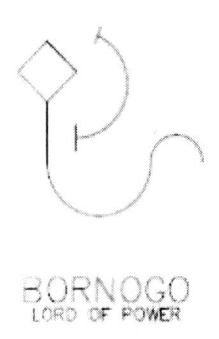

BORNOGO
LORD OF POWER

The Initiation Ritual

"The introduction and initiation of a new member of the coven makes me shutter with grim delight!"

Aleister Nacht

This is the initiation rite of a new member entering the group. The candidate is usually sponsored by an existing Initiate, and this member accompanies the candidate. Multiple inductees may attend the ceremony and accept the charge of the Celebrant. The candidate also undergoes a test of knowledge (relating to what he or she has learned of Temple teachings during the six-month probationary period) and a test of courage. This ceremony may also be amended for a baptismal ritual. One white candle is used and all others are black.

Hooded black robes are worn by all participants except the woman serving as the altar, who is nude. The Initiate(s) are blindfolded and will be brought into the sanctum by two members of the ceremony.

The Celebrant enters the sanctum with the altar and lays her down, spreading her legs widely. The Celebrant will stand between her legs during the ritual.

The ceremony opens with the purification of the air and benediction of the chamber with the phallus. The chalice is filled, but not presented. The four cardinal directions of the compass are invoked with the sword.

The Celebrant then kisses the stomach of the altar, who is in the "prone" (laying down) position. The Celebrant begins his invocation with arms upraised.

Celebrant:

In the name of Satan, Lucifer, Belial, Leviathan, and all the demons, named and nameless, walkers in the velvet darkness, harken to us, O dim and shadowy things, wraith-like, twisted, half-seen creatures, glimpsed beyond the foggy veil of time and space less night. Draw near; attend us on this night of fledgling sovereignty. Welcome a new member, creature of ecstatic, magic light.

Join us in our welcome. With us say: welcome to you, child of joy, product of the dark and musk filled night, ecstasy's delight.

The Initiate's blindfolds are then removed.
The Celebrant turns to the Initiates.

Welcome to you, sorceress (sorcerer), most natural and true magician. Your hands have strength to pull the crumbling vaults of spurious heavens down, and from their shards erect a monument to your own sweet indulgence. Your honesty entitles you to well-deserved dominion o'er a world filled with frightened, cowering men.

The sub deacon hands a lighted black candle to the Celebrant, who passes the flame four times under the outstretched hands of the Initiate, saying:

In the name of Satan, we set your feet upon the Left-Hand Path. Four times above the flame you pass, to kindle lust and passion in your heart, that the heat and brightness of Schamballah's flame may warm you, that your feelings and emotions may burn bright and passionate, to work your magic as you wish. (member's name) , we call you, as your name gleams forth within the flame.

The Celebrant returns the candle to the Sub deacon, who then presents the Celebrant with the bell. The Celebrant rings the bell softly about the initiate. The Celebrant then places the sword on the Initiate's forehead.

Celebrant:
In the name of Lucifer, we ring about you, brightening the air with sounds of tinkling wisdom. As your eyes receive enlightenment, so shall your ears perceive the truth, and separate

Book of Satanic Ritual

life's patterns, that your place will be found. We call your name into the night: O hear sweet (name)'s magic name.

In the name of Belial, we place His mark upon you, to solemnize and etch in memory the dark, moist planet-the Pit from whence you came-the jetting stream of manhood fertilizing Mother Earth. Thus was it always and to time's end will it be. (name), we call you, that your power, too, may last unending, always strong as man and earth, for they are one with thee.

By all the images set forth for childhood's fancy, by all things that creep and shuffle through the faerie fane of night, by all the silken rustles on the wind and croaking in the dark, O frogs and toads and rats and crows and cats and dogs and bats and whales and all you kith and kin of little ones like she (he) who rests before you: bless her (him), sustain her (him), for she (he) is of that which needs no purification, for she (he), like all of you, is perfection in what she (he) is, and the mind that dwells within this head is moved by your god, the Lord of IS, the All-Powerful Manifestation of Satan.

The Celebrant lifts the sword from the Initiate's forehead and, as part of the same gesture, raises its tip up to the Sigil of Baphomet, above and behind the Initiate. All others present face the altar and lift their right arms in the Sign of the Horns.

Celebrant:
Hail, Satan!

All Others:
Hail, Satan!

Celebrant:
Hail, Satan!

All Others:
Hail, Satan!

Celebrant:
Hail, Satan!

All Others:
Hail, Satan!

Celebrant:
It is done. So Mote it be!

All Others:
So Mote it be!

The ceremony is concluded in the usual manner.

Book of Satanic Ritual

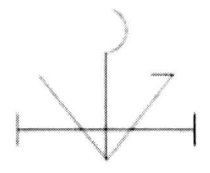

BUTMONO
DEMON OF GREED

Self Initiation Ritual

Set aside an area for the performance of the ritual and in this erect an altar and cover it with a black cloth. The altar may be a table. Obtain some black candles, some candle holders, some hazel incense, a quartz crystal or crystals. You will also need two small squares of parchment (or expensive woven paper), a quill type pen, a sharp knife, some sea salt, a handful of graveyard earth (obtained on a night of the new moon) and a chalice which you should fill with wine. All of these items should be placed on the altar.

Should you wish, you may also obtain a black robe of suitable design. If not, you should dress all in black for the ritual.

An hour before sunset, enter your Temple area, face east and chant the Sanctus Satanas twice. Then say, loudly,

To you, Satan, Prince of Darkness and Lord of the Earth,
I dedicate this Temple: let it become, like my body,
A vessel for your power and an expression of your glory!

Then vibrate 'Agios o Satanas' nine times. After this, take up the salt and sprinkle it over the altar and around the room, saying:

With this salt I seal the power of Satan in!

Take the earth and cast it likewise, saying:

With this earth I dedicate my Temple. Satanas - venire! Satanas venire! Agios O Baphomet! I am god imbued with your glory!

Then light the candles on the altar, burn plentiful incense and leave the Temple. Take a bath, and

Book of Satanic Ritual

then return to the Temple.

Once in the Temple, lightly prick your left forefinger with the knife. With the blood and using the pen inscribe on one parchment the Occult name you have chosen. On the other inscribe an inverted pentagram. Hold both parchments up to the East saying:

With my blood I dedicate the Temple of my life!

Then turn counter *sunwise* three times, saying:

I ...... (state the Occult name you have chosen) am here to begin my sinister quest! Prince of Darkness, hear my oath! Baphomet, Mistress of Earth, hear me! Hear me, you Dark Gods waiting beyond the Abyss!

Burn the parchments in the candles. (Note: it is often more practical to fill a vessel with spirit and place the parchments in this and then set the spirit alight. However if you have chosen woven paper, this method will not be necessary.) As they burn, say:

Book of Satanic Ritual

Satan, may your power mingle with mine as my blood now mingles with fire!

Take up the chalice, raise it to the East, saying:

With this drink I seal my oath. I am yours and shall do works to the glory of your name!

Drain the chalice, extinguish the candles and then depart from the Temple. The Initiation is then complete.

Book of Satanic Ritual

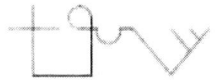

CAMAEL
THE DESTROYER

Concurrent Messes Noirs and Initiation Ritual

Altar Bell (Rung nine times to invoke the spirit Satan.)

Coven (Chanting Invocation)
*"Bagabi laca bachabe Lamac lamec bachalyas
Lamac cahi achababe Cabahagy sabalyos
Karrelyos Baryolos
Lagoz atha cabyolas
Samahac et famyolas
Harrahya"*

Book of Satanic Ritual

High Priest (Enters to center of the altar and chants, while crossing himself in a counterclockwise direction with his left hand)
"In nominee de nostre "In the name of our Satanas: Lucifere Satan; the glorious Excelsis!" Lucifer!"

High Priest (chants)
"Introibo ad alatare "I will go up to the Satanas." Altar of Satan."

Coven (chants)
"Ad Satanas, qui laetificat gloria "To Satan, the giver of youth and glory."

Coven (chants ancient conjuration to yield their souls to the devil)
"Palas aron ozinomas Geheamel cla orlay Baske bano tudan donas Berec he pantaras tay."

High Priest "In the name of Satan, ruler of Earth, the King of the world, the Chief of the Serfs, I command the forces of darkness to bestow their infernal power upon us. Save us, Lord Satan, from the treacherous and the violent. Oh Satan, Spirit of the Earth, God of Liberty, open wide the gates of Hell, And come forth from the abyss by these names:"

High Priest and Coven "Satan! Beelzebub! Leviathon! Asmodeus! Abaddon!"

High Priest (chants)
"Gloria Satanas, et Belial et Spiritui and Belial, and maloso."

Coven (responds)
"As it was in the beginning, is now, and ever shall be, without end. Amen"

High Priest (chants)
"Satan be with you."

Coven (responds)

"And with thy spirit."

High Priest (Calling the coven to prayer)

"Let us pray . . . Urged by our Lord Satan's bidding, and schooled by his infernal ordinance, we make bold to say:"

High Priest and Coven (Recitation of the Lord's Prayer, backwards)
"Amen . . . Evil from us deliver but . . . Temptation into not us lead and . . . Us against trespass who those forgive we as . . . Trespasses our us forgive and . . . Bread daily our day this us give . . . Heaven in is it as earth on . . . Done be will thy . . . Come kingdom thy . . . Name thy be hallowed . . . Heaven in art who . . . Father our."

High Priest
"Children of my office. From high matters I spare the time to preside over this gathering. By the favor of our Lord Satan, I have the power to grant your wishes, should it please me to do so. Waste no moment in unnecessary babbling or you will incur my anger. Now, lift up your heads, and tell me your desires."

(A loud knock at the side door of the Altar Chamber)

High Priest
"Who seeks entry here?"

Assistant Priestess
"One who repents her past heresies and craves to be accepted into the grace of our Master, Satan . . . designated by the Creator. Lord of this World from beginning without end."

High Priest
"Enter, penitent, that you may abase yourself before the only true God."
(Initiate enters, wearing a long white garment, tied at the waist with a cord, ankles are bound in shackles)

"Penitent, the opportunity is offered you to redeem your past . . . Do you desire to take it?"

Assistant Priestess
"Yes."

High Priest
"Are you prepared to serve our Lord Satan with

your whole mind, body, and soul, permitting nothing to deter you from the furtherance of his work?

Initiate
"Yes."

High Priest
"As proof that you have purged your mind of all false teaching, you will now break this crucifix and throw the pieces from you."

High Priest
"Stand up, and raise your left hand! Repeat after me, sentence by sentence, the words I am about to say:

High Priest and Initiate
"I deny Jesus Christ the deceiver . . . and I abjure the Christian faith, holding in contempt all of its works. By the symbol of the Creator, I swear henceforth to be . . . a faithful servant of his most puissant Arch-Angel, the Prince Lucifer . . . whom the Creator designated as His Regent and Lord of

this World. As a being now possessed of a human body in this world, I swear to give my full allegiance to its lawful Master: to worship Him, our Lord Satan and no other; to despise all manmade religions, and to bring contempt to them whenever possible; to undermine the faith of others in such false religions whenever possible; and bring them to the true faith when desirable. I swear to give my mind, body, and soul unreservedly . . . to the furtherance of the designs of our Lord Satan. If I betray my oath, I do now decree to have my throat cut, my tongue and heart torn out . . . and to be buried in the sand of the ocean that the waves of it may carry me away into an eternity of oblivion."

High Priest
"If you ever break this oath, we shall pronounce sentence upon you in the name of our Lord Satan . . . that you shall fall into dangerous disease and leprosy, and that, in the sign of his vengeance, you shall perish by a terrifying and horrible death, and that a fire shall consume and devour you on every side and utterly crush you . . . and that by the power of Satan, a flame shall go forth from

His Mouth which shall burn you up and reduce you to nothing in Hell ..."

High Priest
(Removes a bag from the altar; this bag contains the shavings of a clock)
"Now take these shavings in your hand and face the Goat of Mendes . . . repeat after me:

High Priest and Initiate
"I deny God, Creator of Heaven and Earth, and I adhere to thee, and believe in thee."
High Priest (Leads the Initiate to the right side of the altar to a black throne, upon which is seated Satan in the materialization of a huge black goat with a human body, but with the hooves and head of a goat. The goat has three horns, the middle one being a lighted torch)

"Kiss the Goat!!"

(As the Initiate kisses the posterior of the goat from behind the throne, the ceremony of fidelity to Satan known as the Pax, the High Priest intones)

"As the shavings of the clock do never return to the clock from which they are taken, so may your soul never return to Heaven."

(Leading the Initiate back to the altar)

"Now . . . remove your garment and lie down at full length upon the altar."

(As the Initiate drops the garment and lies naked on the altar, the High Priest stretches out her arms and places a lighted black candle in each outstretched hand. Some members of the assemblage are beginning to express their emotions.)

"Brothers and sisters of the Left-Hand Path . . . the penitent has proved a worthy neophyte in our high order. It is now my happy duty to free her from the bonds of ignorance and superstition." (The High Priest removes the shackles from the ankles of the Initiate and proceeds with the rite symbolic of copulation with the devil. If the Lord

Book of Satanic Ritual

Satan or one of his demons is present at this portion of the Mass, the High Priest will step aside and lead conjurations of lust while the ceremony is actually performed.

After this rite, the Initiate, still serving as the altar, has the Chalice containing the host and a skull filled with blood placed upon her prone body. The host is generally stolen from a Catholic church, dyed black, and cut into a triangular shape.

High Priest (chants)
"Satanas gratias." "Thanks be to Satan"
"Satanas vobiscum." "Satan be with you."

Coven (responds)
"And with thy spirit."

High priest and Coven (Walks to left of human altar to begin the Offertory. He holds up the Paten containing the consecrated host)
"Lucifer, Save us! Master, Save us!
Astaroth, Save us! Master, Save us!
Shaiton, Save us! Master, Save us!
Zabulon, Save us! Master, Save us!

Maloch, Save us! Master, Save us!"

(High Priest walks to the right of human altar, and holds up the skull or other Chalice containing the elixir)
*"Satan, Have mercy! Master, Have mercy!
Baal, Have mercy! Master, Have mercy!
Azazel, Have mercy! Master, Have mercy!
Dagon, Have mercy! Master, Have mercy!
Mammon, Have mercy! Master, Have mercy!"*

High Priest (Taking Communion, consecrates the Paten and the Chalice with the blessing of Death)
"Blessed be the bread and wine of death . . . blessed a thousand times more than the flesh and blood of life, for you have not been harvested by human hands nor did any human creature mill and grind you. It was our Lord Satan who took you to the mill of the grave, so that you should thus become the bread and blood of revelation and revulsion. I spit upon you! And I cast you down! In the memory of Satan, because you preach punishment and shame to those who would emancipate themselves and repudiate the slavery of the church!"

Book of Satanic Ritual

(He casts the consecrated host and blood on the floor in front of the altar and spits on them. At this sign, the entire congregation rushes up amidst screams of hate and tramples upon the mixture. They also scramble and fight for remnants to be used in casting private spells)

High Priest
(Tearing off his vestments and trampling them on the ground . . .)
"These ornaments, badges of authority, serve only to conceal the nakedness which is alone acceptable to our Lord Satan!"

(Entire coven rips off their robes and any other garments amidst bestial shrieks and growls. This is silenced by the High Priest who rings a gong, causing the reaction of a thunder clap. The High Priest holds his left hand aloft helping the unsteady, and seemingly drugged, young Initiate off the altar to stand naked before the now naked coven)

"Initiate, you have served me well! Stand up and

Book of Satanic Ritual

join these assembled here so that they may look upon you, and do with you as they desire ..."

(The Initiate is pushed into the midst of the assemblage.)

High Priest
(Announcing the dismissal from the formal Mass, proclaiming the Benediction for increased virility, and calling for the homage to Satan through feasting, dancing, and a general orgy till dawn)

"I, Prince of Demons and High Priest of the Lord Satan, by this act do dismiss you from this service. Prepare to receive through me the Benediction of Our Lord Satan, that you may honor the Creator by the rite symbolical of his work ..."

(As the altar bell is again rung nine times, the High Priest wanders among the assemblage, touching the genitals of each member of the coven with a special Satanic blessing to insure the success of the orgy to follow. The ritual sex is optional once the mass has ended)

Book of Satanic Ritual

High Priest "
Ave Satanas! Vade Lilith, vade retro Pan! Deus maledictus est!! Gloria tibi! Domine Lucifere, per omnia saecula saeculorum. Amen!!"

"Do What Thou Wilt, Shall Be the Whole of the Law!"

"Rege Satanas! Hail Satan!
Ave Satanas! Hail Satan!
Hail Satan!! Hail Satan!"

Coven
Hail Satan!! Hail Satan!"

The ritual sex orgy begins (optional)

Book of Satanic Ritual

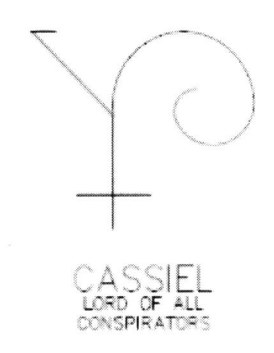

CASSIEL
LORD OF ALL
CONSPIRATORS

Destruction Ritual

In the name of Chaos, Sam-Moveth-Az. Ob-Azoth Lord and Archdemon of Infernus.

I call for the Five Gates of the dark realm to crash asunder. Let my commands ride upon the howling winds of the Abyss.

Oh, Herald of Hell, behold: I speak the Keys of the 9 Angles and I summon the demon who has leashed the apocalypse, Abot-Thiavat, Master of the Seven, whose name is Oblivion.

Through the Blazing Angles of the Shining Trapezoid whereby the 10th Key (Malkuth) lies

broken, the doom of _____ has been spoken.
Eurynome! Cthonie! Callrhoe! Ekidne! Ophioneus!

(Pronounced: (YU-RUH-NO-MEH, KTHO-NEE, KALLIR-OH-EH, EH-KID-NEH, O-FEE-ON-EE-US)
Samael! Azazel! Izidkiel! Hanael! Kepharel!
(The same 5 names, but in Hebrew)
The names have been spoken, loose the Hounds of the Barrier and COME FORTH, for the bond is sealed. We are alike, and I summon you through myself that MY WILL BE DONE! By Sam-Moveth-Az, by Ophioneus: Leviathan, Arise! Move! Appear! Leave the whirling vortex beyond our Cosmos and come forth.

Behold the goat without horns, untouched, alone, naked before you, having only the Black Fire that burns in my heart. I AM the mystery of YOUR creation! Come into my heart and GO FORTH: strike down! rot away! burn up! crush! consume and devour!

Book of Satanic Ritual

Now - FIND the enemy or enemies with your heart chakra (NOT with the head-eye chakra). With the head-eye chakra LOOK as if looking down on many things and BLAST the enemy. It comes out like "go-pause, go-pause, go-pause," it does not blast out like the Vajra. Then break off, become totally detached from this. Even forget you did it! Total detachment.

Explanation:
The 10th Key is Malkuth after Bahu breaks open. Thiavat comes out of this through the middle pillar - or the Abot Gate. The Thiavat-Bahu combined is the Root of the 7 "Light Forces" hence the Master of them (See Dark Kaballa article sold).

Hounds of the Barrier are the Furies, the five Daimones. There is a whirling feeling associated with this magic, and a howling sound or fluty kind of song-howl that one can "hear." Sam-Moveth-Az represents the Obic Vortex above 1st. Ophioneus is what came from the 10th last. Leviathan is the culmination of both, the entire thing. The goat without horns is the person doing the spell meaning that he/she has been harmed or deprived of the horns - metaphorically. Untouched means you do not hold hands with anyone in this spell. Alone means the one person alone does this spell, even if others are present. Naked doesn't have to mean you disrobe but you can - it means INNOCENT of motive, pure of heart - it means you have nothing anymore except the Black Flame which is the Self Alone.

The epithets 1. strike down, 2. rot away, 3. burn up 4. crush and 5. consume devour - that is how the Thiavat-as-Ob comes down through the Vortex through middle pillar. These are the attributes of the Seraphim punishing, wrathful messengers. Guardians of the Five Gates.

Tipereth is passed through which is the heart wherein the Black Fire burns. You call this into your HEART and send it forth as the spell reads. Blazing Angles of the Trapezoid are the 7-light forces with the dark inside as shown in "Tantra" article. Crash through the 9 angles: 5 on the star the alphas/points plus four on the trapezoid seem to crush inward - the 4 on the trapezoid are the Tetragrammaton - and have nothing to do with any "name of God."

Book of Satanic Ritual

Ritual of Baphomet

1) Stand facing any preferred Direction

2) Inhale fully. Exhale slowly sustaining the sound "I" (a high-pitched ieeeeee! Sound) while visualizing a dark energy in the head area.

3) Inhale fully. Exhale slowly sustaining the sound "E" (a lower-pitched eeeeh! Sound) while visualizing a dark energy in the throat area.

4) Inhale fully. Exhale slowly sustaining the Sound "A" (a deep aaaah! Sound) while visualizing a dark energy in the heart and lungs, which spreads to the muscles of the limbs.

5) As in 2, but the "O" sound (ooooh!) in the belly area.

6) As in 2, but the Sound "U" (a very deep uuur!) in the Genital/anal area.

Book of Satanic Ritual

7) Repeat 6. Then 5, 4, 3, 2, working back toward the head.

8) Trace the Inverted Pentagram before you like this (either actually trace it on a floor, or trace it in your mind's eye by using an arm gesture. If you are actually walking on the star, walk to each next point as shown in the diagram. If you are doing it in your mind's eye, step to the left each time in a circular way. SAY:

"SAMAEL"
9) Move to the next point or step left. Trace the Inverted Pentagram (as shown in Drawing) before you and say:

"LUCIFER"
10) Move to next point or to your left. Trace the Inverted Pentagram before you and say:

"SATAN"
11) Move to next point or to your left. Trace the Inverted Pentagram before you and say:

Book of Satanic Ritual

"AZAZEL"
12) Move to next point or to your left. Trace the Inverted Pentagram before you and say:

"LEVIATHAN"
13) Either face the pentagon in the center of the star and walk into it, facing the two top points, or move left again. With arms stretched out say:

"Before me to my right SAMAEL
Before me to my left AZAZEL
Beside me on my left LUCIFER
Beside me on my right SATAN
Behind me LEVIATHAN"
"About me flames the star of the BAPHOMET the ALL-Mother/Father! Within me burns the Black Flame of vital fire!"

14) Repeat steps 2 to 7

Ritual of Black Flame

You will need a bell and a cup of wine (or water). Walking around in a circle going counter

Book of Satanic Ritual

clockwise, ring bell. 9 times.

Perform the entire Ritual of Baphomet

Then say:

"Behold! The earth, my dwelling, My place of pleasure and pain. I am here to acknowledge my bond with it and its ways...the carnal laws of man...truth!"
"I am here this day to proclaim my life to the gift and power of the Beast, the beast within me...the true Self!"

Ring bell

"I call forth my inner black flame from the five angles of our Sign, our Ancient Glyph"

Facing the top right point of the pentacle:
"The Guardian of Angle of the Gate, the Source of my material being, the place of my dwelling and of the earth. I call forth Samael"

Ring bell.

Book of Satanic Ritual

Facing the top left point of the pentacle:

The Guardian of the Angle of The Flame, the Spark in the Eye of the Great Darkness, the place of my heart, I call forth Azazel!"

Ring bell.
Facing lower left point of the pentacle:

"The Guardian of the Angle of Light and of air, the force of my breath, the abode of the enlightened one, I call forth Lucifer"

Ring bell.
Facing the lower right point of pentacle:

"The Guardian of the Angle of the unholy fire, the inner flame of indulgence, the abode of the dark prince. I call forth Satan!"

Ring bell.
Facing the lower point of the pentacle:
"The Guardian of the angle of the deep sea...the rushing serpent. The place of my creation and the Root of my Being. I call forth Leviathan"

Ring bell.

"And above me, the might and glory above all else, The Self! Humanity in its glory, I am a true manifestation of its greatness. Shemhemphorash! Hail thyself! I am here to realize and bless myself in the Black Flame of truth. I am here to deliver myself from false belief and self-deceit, I am here to open the path to my carnal nature."
"I, a beast of the field, a being of flesh, proclaim myself a Satanist"
"I reject all false knowledge and self-deceit"
"I live life for myself and those I love"

Drink from the Cup of Water (or Wine): and Say

"I partake of this blessing, I am made strong with this carnal mixture, in the name of the Five whose Angles the Pentacle do make, and all the Gods of the Outer Darkness. I am empowered by the inner black flame. I walk forth into the world and partake of my desires and true nature. Shemhemphorash, hail thyself!"

Book of Satanic Ritual

Perform the Ritual of Baphomet again

"It is done"

Ring bell 9 times to close.

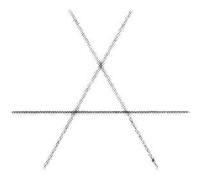

DIGDIN
THE DISORDERED

PART III

In the world of Satanism, opposites play a role in the everyday following of the Left Hand Path. Anton LaVey wrote in The Satanic Rituals; "On the altar of the Devil up is down, pleasure is pain, darkness is light, slavery is freedom, and madness is sanity. The Satanic ritual chamber is the ideal setting for the entertainment of unspoken thoughts or a veritable palace of perversity"

Opposites, as any opposition, are direct polar extremes. In the case of a magnet, the polar opposites actually create a great source of power. Opposition in human life is, for the Satanist, a good thing. We learn to sharpen our energy forces and hone them into a force that can change reality. "Perception is reality" and the perception your adversary is under will be of great benefit to you in any oppositional situation.

Simply put, this defines magic. Altering reality becomes the reality and moving the energy as you wish is the greatest of all magical processes for the Satanist. This is not something you can acquire overnight and certainly you cannot create knowledge from ignorance without a change in motivation and behavior. The ancient sorcerers practiced the Satanic arts and learned how to channel the energy needed to change the perception (and circumstances) of scenarios while recording their experimental operations in grimoires. Learning "what worked and what did not work" was the most critical step in the process for without it, the magical processes would simply become futile repetitions. The result must be accepted prima facie.

A human will never know more that what 1) they are exposed to or 2) what is taken in through one of the five senses. There is no such thing as spontaneous knowledge. If you have entered Satanism searching for knowledge, you will learn if you open yourself to experience "Satanism".

Book of Satanic Ritual

You must be willing to invest in your objective and relentlessly pursue Satanic knowledge for without this, you will waste your time.

While opposites can attract, it is the skilled practitioner that can harness the magical energy in such a way that two changes simultaneously result; Perception Change and Reality Change. During a magical working, the coven attempts to leverage the strengths of the group as they minimize the weaknesses............and yes, even Satanists with LARGE EGOS have weaknesses.

Note: Quite often, their huge ego is their weakness; allowing them to be guided as a sheep to the proverbial slaughter.

Perception can be changed simply by moving the variables of the cognitive landscape around to rearrange them to your satisfaction. Women wear makeup, wear high heels and change their hairstyle to change perception...........the way they are perceived. Men color their hair, drive a sports car and brags about the woman he had sex with last night. This changes people's perception. In Satanism, as in magic, changing perception works the same way but must be accomplished through process. If you are placing a spell on the man / woman you desire, you will use magical operations during the ritual to make them more open and receptive to your advances or you may simply want their attention and let the change of reality "close the deal".

At the same time, the ritual serves as a vehicle through which reality may be changed in order for you to gain an advantage; whatever that may be. Again, the operations of the ritual will allow you to change reality and reap the benefits such as calling that man / woman "yours". These spells and rituals are powerful for the competent Satanist who can learn from the Satanic grimoires created long ago.

Change is everywhere in the world and the Satanist must accept an ever-changing magical topography. The Satanist will always be subjected to changes in magic, energy, coven, lifestyle, fiscal position, etc. because that is the pure nature of magic. Many of the sorcerers of old were nomadic (usually due to following the migration of their prime food sources) and thus the stigma of gypsies and those forever wandering and roaming the earth was created.

Because we as Satanists live in continuous change,

we can (and often do) take advantage of those changes happening around us. Humans are "creatures of habit" and adapting to change allows the Satanist to take advantage of the chaos that usually ensues during times of change. Zeroing in on those who do not cope well with change will allow the practitioner to exploit that characteristic magically. If you know *"_____ will cause _____ to happen"*, you are now controlling the variables in what can often be a very complex situation. Take advantage of the confusion and uncertainty that comes with the changes and you will be in a better position to get what you want through magical ritual operations.

It has been said that Nostradamus was a brilliant prophet and through his knowledge of the celestial bodies allowed him to foretell some of the most important events in the history of man. Others have claimed he was an inept astrologer, artless without aesthetic aptitude, incompetent, maladroit and above all, a plagiarist. It is common knowledge that Nostradamus "lifted" many things he wrote from other books and other authors. What is interesting: most people recognize the name Nostradamus while very, very few would recognize the names of those authors he "borrowed" his ideas from. Say what you may but he certainly carved himself a place in history and a legacy that lives on even today.

Nostradamus wrote about diabolical subjects, controversial ideas and prophesies that are still being interpreted by scholars. He embraced the idea of human suffering on an epic scale in his 942 Quatrains. Gloom and doom always sell but he took the writing a step further by actually making the reader "invest themselves" in the writings. These events would happen to people, just like the reader and this connected the reader to the subject matter the same way an American might become emotionally invested while reading the accounts of 9/11. Nostradamus found his niche and worked diligently to write about many different subjects within the context of foretelling the future. Thus, he will be known forever.

The Satanist must use the same approach to magic. He / she must learn, practice, record and repeat over again in order to build their competency. Nostradamus may not have been able to foretell the future but no one can deny he knew how to write!

Anyone who has read my books or visited Aleister Nacht.com knows that I love women. I also know women can become some of the strongest Satanic practitioners of magic. Those willing to apply themselves can become powerful, manipulative and magically competent allowing them to realize their deepest desires through magical process and application.

Magistra Templi Rex Blanche Barton had this to say about the female Satanist:

"The smartest, most passionate, most beautiful women I've met have been Satanists. I don't mean "beautiful on the inside where it really counts;" I mean gorgeous, vibrant, curvy women. Most non-Satanic men find Satanic women intimidating – too intelligent or too pretty, or worse yet, both at the same time. It takes a special woman to be a Satanist. Only the most truly liberated are summoned to Satan's legions. Up until quite recently, the ratio of Satanic men to women had been about 10 to 1, but that seems to be shifting. More and more young women are going through the process of exploring feminism and Wicca, seeking feminine pride, identity and power, and discovering only impotence,

limitations and puritanical self-righteousness. Wicca and feminism share a flaccid, lackluster attitude and presentation. Satanic women like drama/adventure and know how to conjure it for themselves. Satanists have an innate complexity of mind that hungers for uncompromising examination and speculation, not superficially comforting pap. We don't need to be comforted; we prefer the invigorating, bracing winds of truth and terror."

I agree with this statement. The Satanic woman can open the doorway to control, power, respect, attraction and if she so desires……….her enemies will tremble with fear. I have had the pleasure of attending rituals with some of the women described above and they are unquestionably some of the most magically powerful Satanists I have ever had the pleasure of meeting. A female Satanist with her mind in the right place and well prepared is an awesome "force of nature". Hail Satan!!!

MICZARIEL
THE WARRIORESS

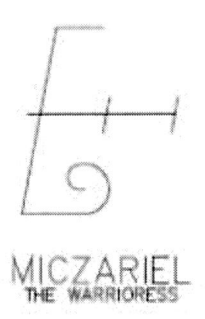

Ritual Preparation

I have written many posts on ritual preparation and I cover all aspects of Satanic magic in my book; *Book of Satanic Magic*. One aspect of ritual preparation is the cleansing of the body; internally and externally. Opening one's self to internal cleansing enables the practitioner to expel any stored negative energy while removing any blockages to the Chakras of the body.

The external cleansing is accomplished by bathing and is an important demonstration of respect for the demon(s) that are to be summoned and Satan himself. The cleaning of the physical body also shows respect to other coven members who participate in sexually oriented rituals requiring certain "acts" to be performed in order to increase Satanic energy to be used. I discuss how this works in several books. Satanic Sex Magic uses the powerful climatic energy to be sent into the atmosphere where it accompanies the magical operation (and often a demon) to accomplish the practitioner's desires.

Two or three hours before the actual ritual begins, I often invite one or two coven members to shower with me as a part of the ritual preparation. For me, having the opportunity to bath with a woman (or women) is a very sensual, erotic and enjoyable event in preparation for a ritual. There is a connection between us since we are becoming in tune with not only the approaching ritual but with our bodies also. The objective is not to have sex; that will come later at the ritual. The objective is to arouse one another slowly to create energy that will be released later during the ritual.

MURIEL
GREAT DEMON OF LIES

Free Thinkers

I want to do bad things with you..........
Satanic ritual is very important and enhancing the performance of ritual is paramount to the magical flow of energy. Ritual is, in fact, what makes the magic happen. Without ritual or without taking the time to make a ritual satisfactory to Satan, you can only expect failure.

I have tried to clarify these points in previous books. I believe that, given the past and my experience, I can speak intelligently concerning the black arts and more especially, Satanic ritual. I receive a lot of correspondence and many times people are simply looking for a magical way of short cutting their way into the black blessings of Satan. In order to receive those blessings from the hell you must be willing to open those gates of hell and that means inviting those who will help you in such a Satanic endeavor.

This is the essence of magic for without ritual, magic will not happen and without adequate preparation, the ritual will be ineffective and ineffective rituals equal wasted time and energy. Also, without knowing the outcome of the ritual and without planning a ritual to take place at a certain time, date and in a certain manner then you can only expect failure. Satan is looking for those who have the knowledge, wisdom, endurance and fortitude to see a ritual through to its logical end. For without the ritual, magic will not happen and this is a fact.

When first beginning the ritual, harnessing the energy current is probably the most important step. Satan (or any measure of demons) may manifest during your ritual; especially if you invoke those spirits directly however, if you do not invite these beings into your ritual you are simply setting yourself up for failure. For how can magic truly work with out a transcendent messenger to deliver that magic in your behalf. Binding spells and incantations are important to be performed by the Satanic and they must be performed to the prescription or specification required to deliver that all-important energy. Satan nor his demons will respect a person who cannot or will not properly perform a Satanic ritual.

Free Spirits (aka Free Thinkers) roam the earthly realm seeking satisfaction for a longing that resembles an unquenchable thirst. Free Spirits explore possible answers to questions of the entire universe. These brave souls often encounter ridicule, jeering, aspersion, verbal (sometimes physical) attacks and other threats because they ask one question that irritates those liars hoping to sell falsity and through vituperation to the masses..........the question..........."Why?".

The word is miniscule and quite trivial until asked at the right time and place. Used correctly, the word can bring the most powerful person to their knees; or at least make them run like HELL. It can put the fear of SATAN in a person and it cannot be circumvented if crafted by a skilled orator. It opens any subject for microscopic – diminutive scrutiny and can reveal shortcomings and the metaphorical "cracks under the paint".

I have also seen Free Spirits destroy a Satanic coven that was based upon and practicing "Bullshit rituals created by a bullshit artist pretending to be a Satanic Magus". One Free Spirit brought that coven to its end by simply asking "Why?". It is a double-edged sword that can very well cut right through the pretension and reveal truth and motives.

The Free Spirit can destroy almost at will. In the eyes of established religion, a Free Spirit is "dangerous" and while the established church may take a stance of approachability, the church is very afraid of the Free Spirit. One thinker in a group can soon discredit a liar, con artist and / or prevarication. Yes, one person can hold the power of an entire army and the established church know that all too well.

Throughout history, Free Spirits have formed public opinion once a viable communication medium was made available. The truth is not always "good news" and sometimes those who shout for the truth are the ones that try to stifle the message from being accessible to the masses. If a Free Spirit challenges the idea or opinion of someone well "impacted" in a powerful organization, it can be a bitter pill for the Free Spirit.

For example, Paganism had a great influence on developing Christianity, unknown to many today practicing the Christian faith. The cult of Isis and Osiris first spoke of rebirth and resurrection, cornerstones in Christianity. The images of Jesus on Mary's lap was co-opted from that of Isis holding her son, Horus. The Cult of the Virgin was influenced by the more ancient Goddesses: Isis, Demeter and Artemis, with Mary sharing some of these Goddess' epithets. No one can accurately cite Jesus' actual birth date so Church officials in a very calculated move, chose December 25th, a date first associated with pagan holy days. In another move to convert pagans to Christianity, the Church closed pagan temples and opened churches on the same sacred sites of pagan deities.

A Free Spirit would certainly understand, and after due diligence, accept the statement above if there existed corroborating evidence and verifiable sources verified. A Christian would, almost certainly, rebut the statement and attempt to discredit the Free Spirit, thus turning the attention of bystanders to that of the Free Spirit instead of the issue at hand. This is a defensive tactic called "redirection" and it is used extensively by the church today. One only has to challenge a long-standing Christian belief to see the tactic in action. Sorry, I go off of the subject.

Be a Free Spirit for Satanism. Always ask questions and never settle for a lie when the truth would be so much more liberating.

NABERIUS
LORD OF CUNNING

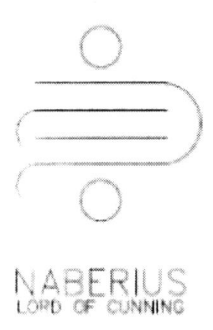

Demonic Forces

All Demons are not evils just as all Angels are not good. Shakespeare said it best 400 years ago: "There's nothing to fear but fear itself" and "Hell is empty; all the devils are here".

There have been countless reported demonic possessions throughout history. Some are legitimate and substantiated however most are not. In most cases there can be found a clinical or other explanation for what is called "possession". As our civilization becomes more educated and open-minded concerning possession, the more cases are dismissed as what they truly are: physical / mental illnesses, drug abuse or other rationality.

Book of Satanic Ritual

There are however, those events that do not fit neatly into one or more of these diagnosis and are categorized as Demonic / Satanic Possession.

The unraveling of the human psyche is a frightening happening when mixed with demons. Possession however, is not always a theatrical affair nor is it as portrayed in the movie The Exorcist.

Believe it or not, demons prefer to be invited guests and usually wait for the host to extend an invitation through ritual or other magical device. Demons can possess the unwilling host but it is usually preempted by the host performing some act that may be misconstrued as an invitation. This can happen through Familiars as discussed during Part 2 of those series.

Opening one's self to the Satanic or Demonic forces is a serious matter and should be treated as such. In popular culture, the Ouija board has played a big part in the opening of the host in preparation for possession. When a person opens themselves and subjects their mind and body to the being, the process is set into motion. Whether intentionally or not, once the chain of events are set into motion, the script must be played out on the stage that is everyday life. Occult "dabblers" are many times the guinea pigs for the strong demonic forces.

A big mistake "dabblers" make is underestimation of demonic power and energy that can be easily wielded by a being. I equate this force to a riptide. No matter how hard you flight to swim against the riptide, you will only exhaust all your energy before being carried out to sea or drowned. Once in the grip of the force, not even a brisance will break the force. Abject consequences will surely await the dabblers. Evil can be a fierce power and the wage for calling it forth can be too high to pay for the ignorant or unprepared.

The case of Anneliese Michel is usually referenced by those trying to prove or disprove possession. The case has been labeled by some as mental illness, negligence, abuse, and religious hysteria. She suffered from epilepsy and was treated at several clinics in Germany during the late sixties and early seventies. A devout Catholic, Michel began to attribute her condition to demonic possession. Michel became intolerant of sacred places and objects, such as the crucifix, which she attributed to her own demonic possession.

Once convinced of her possession, Anneliese, her

parents, and the exorcist stopped seeking medical treatment, and put her fate solely into the hands of the exorcism rites. Sixty-seven exorcism sessions, one or two each week, lasting up to four hours, were performed over about ten months in 1975 and 1976. On 1 July 1976, Anneliese died in her sleep.

Such events have been sensationalized in the media as possessions however, most have a logical explanation that does not include demons or Satan. Possession is much more subdued that most people believe and while a person vomiting Pea Soup is more entertaining, the fact is most of the wrestling of good and evil takes place within the brain of the possessed. This is more dangerous that physical manifestations because it is hard to diagnose that which cannot be seen. It is no doubt that some people committing unspeakable acts upon humanity are in fact demonically possessed; not all but some.

A skilled magician can invite demons to inhabit them while performing rituals and spells. Preparation is important and knowledge of the Demonic and Satanic is required to achieve success.

OZGIN
DEMON OF MADNESS

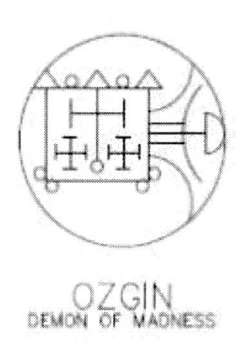

The Familiar

"Familiar - In Western demonology, small animal or imp kept as a witch's attendant, given to her by the devil or inherited from another witch. The familiar was a low-ranking demon that assumed any animal shape, such as a toad, dog, insect, or black cat.

Sometimes the familiar was described as a grotesque creature of fantasy, an amalgam of several creatures. The familiar was believed to subsist by sucking blood from a witch's fingers or other protuberances on her body such as a mole or a wart. During the European witchcraft trials of the 15th–17th century a suspected witch was searched for the "teats" by which she fed her familiar, and these, like the devil's brand marks, were considered sure signs of her guilt."

A conversation of Demonic Possession often turns to the topic of "Familiars" and quite honestly, most people have no idea what Familiars are or what role they are said to play in Demonology or the Satanic. I wanted to touch upon this in my Demonic Possession series since I have received emails with such inquiries. Let's get started, shall we?

As stated in Britannica's definition of Familiar we find that some of the folklore of Halloween was taken from the Familiar. The representation of black cats, toads and other creatures can certainly been seen a few weeks before Halloween on any isle of Target, Wal-Mart, Costco, etc. Now, before the conspiracy theorists (or Christians) invent a new story that all retailers are worshiping the devil, let's just remember that consumers drive what is offered for sale in a retail store. These businesses are not holding Satanic rituals in the back of the store to ensure the Captain Jack Sparrow mask will sell…………Disney perhaps, but not the other retailers.

Most of us enjoy being "safely" scared from time to time. Take for instance the Ferris Wheel or Roller Coaster at the fair or amusement park. We want to be pushed outside of our comfort zone however, no one wants to die as a result. If death was the object, the Captain Sparrow sword would have a stainless steel blade instead of a plastic one.

Since we want to feel afraid, we seek out those things that will create the feeling we desire. Familiars are just that; objects (even people or animals) that create the desired feeling. It is the same thing that makes us want to be around people of like-mindedness and of the same social status and beliefs. We do not want to hang around people who do not inspire, educate, fulfill or otherwise satisfy us in some manner. We want to surround ourselves with................Familiars.

Familiars also come with a built-in attribute of which may sometimes be very difficult to disassociate ourselves. For us, the Familiar carries strong feelings of attachment and reliance; two attributes that are very difficult to control in the human psyche.

For example, if you smoke a cigarette when you

drink alcohol, and you wish to stop smoking, it may be very difficult to resist the urge to smoke while drinking in the future..........especially initially. The same thing may hold true if you smoke a cigarette with your first cup of coffee in the morning. If you stop smoking, that morning coffee will certainly "call for a cigarette" in your subconscious every morning until something else fills that void in the collective psyche.

The Familiars are extremely strong for a drug addict who is trying to quit their addiction. The person who supplies their drug of choice, the places they usually get their fix and the smell, taste, etc. all combine to make quitting a very difficult endeavor. The addict is encouraged to change their lifestyle, including dissociation with dealers, locations and other things that remind them of the "high" experienced. No witches, toads or spooky things................just psychological "rewiring" of the mind. Simply put, the Familiars must be replaced and avoided in the future to prevent relapse.

From the standpoint of demonic possession, the Familiars are just as important. From the priest wishing to banish a demon, to the coven trying to extend an invitation to the beings well beyond the grasps of earth, knowledge of the associated Familiars is equally needed and desired. For the priest who is working from the Rituale Romanum, identifying and removing the Familiars will aid in breaking the cognitive connection between possessed and possessor. For the coven attempting to attract demons, Familiars are used with equal vigor. The Satanically blessed sacraments and implements of ritual will assist in focusing the energy and will also remove the spiritual languor by creating a focal point for that energy, thus producing the desired results.

Using or omitting Familiars is an important aspect of Demonology and Satanism. Role-play while using Familiars is a powerful aesthetic and theatrical method for opening the mind further to the subconscious and delving into the spiritual dimension.

NOTE: It does not involve a breast-feed imp or a witch with sore nipples
sagging boobs............unless those are your specific Familiars!

Book of Satanic Ritual

Book of Satanic Ritual

PAIMON
MASTER OF INFERNAL CEREMONIES

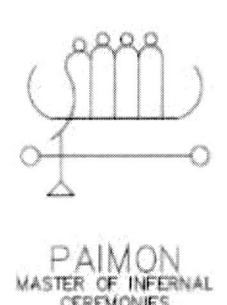

Rituale Romanum

As I have said before "Satan and Demons are real anthropomorphic beings". I know some people will never believe in demons however, once seen and experienced the first time, a person's viewpoint changes forever. If you are reading this post while thinking "Yea right, demons are not real." then you have never experienced the phenomenon for yourself. Whether you are a Christian, Jew, Atheist, Satanist or anything in between, if you do not have first hand experience with demons, you are not qualified to speak or write on the matter............PERIOD!
In the my book titled "Rituale Romanum – The

Exorcist's Handbook", it is explained how the Catholic Church admits their belief in demonic possession but writing, publishing and currently using the document as a process manual with an entire section on exorcism. Why would the church write a book such as the Rituale Romanum if they do not believe possession actually takes place?

"The Rite of Exorcism is not just sanctioned by the local parishes but certain section of the Rituale Romanum are figuratively redacted by the Vatican by including the following statement in the associated sections: "The texts of the Rite of Exorcism are restricted to the study and use of Exorcist Priests who perform this ministry under the direction of the Diocesan Bishop". In keeping with the Hocus Pocus line of thought and the conspiracy theorists' revelation, the church actually refuses to officially reduce the selected section to writing and thus, the priest must have a "fail-safe" type of mission briefing to properly prepare for waging cognitive warfare on the demons of the Satanic Pit."

In the Christian Bible, the Christ performs an exorcism by casting out demons from the

Book of Satanic Ritual

possessed. Whether you believe the events in the bible actually happened or not, there is certainly a precedent set (stare decisis) beginning in those written words concerning demonic possession.

For those who have analyzed William Friedkin's visual interpretation of the William Peter Blatty book "The Exorcist", you should know that a broad artistic license was applied to the movie and while some parts are accurate, other parts are just for aesthetic purposes. For example, I have seen demons hurt people but I have never seen the demon cause cuts, disfigurement or other physical injuries to the demon's host. It does not happen that way and while the host will experience much discomfort during and after the possession, the host is never disfigured.

Another point: "Demons seek those who seek demons". That is right; a person who is dabbling with demons is more likely (and susceptible) to demonic possession than someone taking preventive steps using education, preparation and common sense. I often correspond with those seeking to "conjure a demon" and while this is certainly an admirable thing to aspire to, if they do not know what they are doing they may

Book of Satanic Ritual

unwittingly open the gates of hell and unleash a demon that is "not so willing to assist in magical endeavors". If you wish to use my books to conjure demons, I would advise you to take precautions and educate yourself before an attempt is made. Caveat Emptor…………..

Book of Satanic Ritual

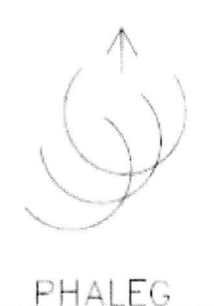

PHALEG
DEMON OF DISCONTENT

Satanic Top 10 List: How to Improve Your Satanic Magic Rituals

People are fascinated with Top 10 lists so I thought I would offer a Satanic Top 10 List: How to Improve Your Satanic Magic Rituals. Since I often answer questions concerning this matter, let's get started.

Number 10: Expect Results

I am surprised how many practitioners do not seriously imagine or expect results from their workings. Why not? The ritual is done in vain without a clear objective.

Number 9: Believe

When a ritual is performed you must not only expect something to happen but you must believe it will happen. One without the other equals wasted time.

Number 8: Plan and Prepare

You need to put some thought into the ritual and you need to know the direction of the magical working. Order is beneficial except when madness and chaos are needed. Write your spells, hexes, etc. and even a script if you desire. Your working will flow much easier and you will make the most efficient use of your time.

Number 7: Bless Your Body

Hygiene is important to the black arts during rituals……..it shows respect to the beings you are inviting. It is also more pleasing to everyone after the ceremony that may partake of fleshly pleasures.

Number 6: Bless Your Temple

Cleaning your temple or sanctum is another form of respect. Good housecleaning aside, arranging the altar, candles, etc. will also allow for a smooth ceremony. You should focus on the magic instead of tripping over a candle holder or other sacramental object. Ensure you have everything needed for the ritual.

Number 5: Create Groupthink

You should discuss and formulate a plan with the group as to what to expect. This goes well with Number 9 and 10.

Number 4: Prepare Initiates

While theatre and visual impact should play a part with Initiates, be sure you give them a short reassurance that everyone goes through an initiation and no one is there to intentionally

Book of Satanic Ritual

hurt them. They are becoming a Satanic coven brother or sister and the night will be remembered for years to come.

Number 3: Open Your Will

As a group, you should open your will to all the Demons of Hell and Satan Himself. Whatever is desired should be fulfilled if at all possible during the ritual. Do not hold back; let yourself go.

Number 2: Focus

You have planned, imagined and now you are expecting results. When it begins to unfold before you, DO NOT STOP! You do not want to suffer from magical Coitus Interruptus........keep the ceremony going on plan and do not stop unless the being commands you.

Number 1: Document

Document the ritual in your Satanic Grimoire for later study and review. Your magic will become better and stronger when you learn what worked well and what did not. You should also take a moment to personally thank the being(s) that graced your working. This instills favor to return to your group during the future.

Following these simple steps will help you achieve new heights in your Satanic Rituals, spells, hexes, etc.

Book of Satanic Ritual

Book of Satanic Ritual

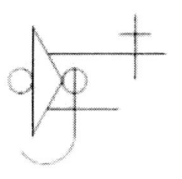

RAUYM
DEMON OF FILTH

Amuse-Bouche

I enjoy writing in phrases using small tasty bits and morsels; I believe the reader should exercise the 'ole noggin to put some things together for their enlightenment. While riddles are too "vague" for me, I do prefer a hint of obscurity. Only those poor impatient souls who believe they are late for their "destiny" are so quick to want the ending of the story prematurely revealed. My Book of Satanic Magic is probably the most forthcoming book I have written.

I am often contacted by readers that feel time is of the essence and they proceed to take a hurried approach and seem to want me to regurgitate the answers to their questions without one thought, hesitation or without vetting them as a legitimate soul seeking real assistance or a vile imp seeking to attempt to trip me with my own words. Yes, there are those antipodes wishing to make themselves seem intelligent by public humiliation of the true and knowledgeable. I am not immune to these bigoted deceivers, theological malingering and games so to help those truly needing help, all must go through a vetting process.

I prefer the Socratic method of teaching; it leads the dialectical student to the answer as a normal progression and it teaches the student to "learn to learn". If this sounds confusing, consider the fact that many people prefer to be told what to believe much more that discovering the truth on their own. My case in point: the Christian Church. I will not flog that dying horse during this post so……..back to the subject.

Some disagreements are positive "brainstorming" methods and as long as the communication channels remain open and both parties continue their dialectical volley, the answer will become more clear with each discussion. To find a solution that results in a "win-win" situation should be the ultimate objective.

I have visited some "Satanic" websites and forums that are total bullshit concerning Satanism. No intelligent ideas are exchanged; people are afraid to submit ideas because the administrators not only take an immediate antithesis but they belittle and humiliate the person to the point that other so-called members join the bandwagon with crude comments and personal attacks. Their forum is nothing more that misguided pontificating and a group of moronic simpletons waving the El Diablo (Mano Cornuto) while chanting "Hail Satan". The very idea that Satan would allow these dim-witted imbeciles into HIS court is neither laughable nor trivial. What these obtuse, misguided fools do not understand is "they are harming themselves and a byproduct of their stupidity". Satan will not be mocked. HE will let these individuals take as much rope as they need to put around their pathetic necks. I, once again, digress.

I also experience the young ladies who want to symbolically (or realistically) fuck their way to Satanic understanding…….a type of "teacher's pet" approach. As most people know, I do have a weakness for women; always have and always will. I do enjoy the touch, taste, smell and other attributes of the fairer sex. There are wonderful and beautiful women out there; I receive nude pics of them on a weekly basis and I love to lust for each one. All women have a certain quality that sets them apart from the others and makes them "tantalizing". I love the attention. It is as close as I will ever be to a Rock Star.

While the offering is great and flattering, a woman should understand that she must take the Satanic Arts seriously and that does not mean she needs to prostitute herself in order to gain knowledge. Other religions limit the tasks or stations a woman can hold within the organization however, Satanism does not limit the woman in any way. Everyone is encouraged to broaden their horizons and learn as much as possible. Religions that limit the "sacred knowledge" to a few should raise a RED FLAG immediately for someone considering joining their fold. Satanism does not seek to stifle learning………………if the leader tries, you should LEAVE THE GROUP IMMEDIATELY!!!!!

I derive a great deal of satisfaction from assisting

those truly attempting to learn the Satanic arts. In some instances, I actually force myself to see things through their eyes and understand not only where they are coming from but where they are going. I have even developed relationships that brought the person into our affiliated coven. For me, this is a wonderful reward.

I encourage you, the reader, to challenge yourself to gain a deeper understanding of the Dark Arts. Small pieces of information, as succulent as an amuse-bouche, is awaiting you. Unlock the secrets and seek to educate yourself by formulating your own beliefs as a result of diligent and intelligent research.

Bon Appétit..................

Book of Satanic Ritual

Book of Satanic Ritual

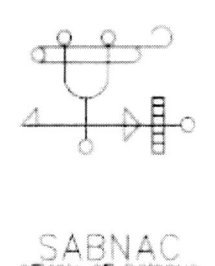

SABNAC
DEMON OF POISONS

Sic Luceat Lux............

Everyone wants to know something no one else knows. Knowledge is power. To know the ending of a story, the punch line of a joke or the winner of a contest before the end is powerful and awe-inspiring. Good and evil have much in common and yet they are separated by excuses and banter. Both have secrets and both have locks of which only the keys of knowledge will open. From the womb to the grave, the quest for the powerful and double-edged sword of silence is found and forgotten. Blood is shed and lives snuffed out in the parcel of time dedicated to that one penchant event. Hate finds love and death awakes in the grave.

When will the last exhaled breath be surrendered and the other side embraced and accepted? Death is waiting for all of us and the truncation of hours to seconds will not abate the inevitable. Silence is golden however it can also be the death of an organization. Without the flow of energy the order becomes stagnate and novelty wears thin.

Satanism is a prime example.

Youth and vitality are attributes that are coveted throughout the world. Young men are viewed as able to pass the seed of life on in the never-ending cycle. Young women are viewed as "fresh"; their luscious breasts promising ample nutrition for newborns and her wet cleft dripping with desire. She can create and foster the future. She can calm the rage. Through her numerous pulsating orgasms she invites the semen of the warrior into her private space of which she only shares with the one whom she chooses her heart to share. Entering her is so exciting.

The members chant and the air grows thick with energy.

Verses are read and the answers of many call out

in repeat. The candles are the only although there is plenty illumination for our tasks at hand this night. Demons roaming the earth have solace and a home with us as the moon cuts through the curtain of night. Come in and join us.

We are going about the Father's work.

The smell of incense fills the air. Our temple, our worshipful unholy void in the vastness of emptiness and we fill it with cries of pain and joy. We create a frenzy of lusts and invite evil to lay on our altar. Fate is the absence of direction; a truly causeless journey for cowards. We know what we do; what we say………..we are proud that we can offer the most precious of the young skin, so white and pale – barely a blemish on the canvas we are about to paint with our fallen fluids.

Bound at the four corners to secure the inevitable. The secret she came seeking and tonight she shall know us all.

Into our club we welcome her and into our family we abide and present to our quorum. I lick my lips and the bell sounds of the 9th. Open the chest with the air of shouting and claim the darkness for it belongs to us; HIS children. We fall into Satanic ecstasy and the smell of her floats on the heated

Book of Satanic Ritual

air of the candles. I love you Athame............I will hold you tightly tonight. With precision you shall allow us to partake of great energy for WE ARE GODS! Across the neck of shame do I place my blade; you do not intimidate our child and we will stand tall and ring the Satanic bell.

In Nomine Dei Nostri Satanas, Luciferi Excelsi..............

My eyes are as open doors for the concupiscence of her.........I can barely hold my impious motivations. My robe warms with craving. My sword is as forged steel and my hands are impatient for the entropy of ritual and benedictions. The silk glides smoothly over my scepter. A thin line of "dew of lecherous fissure" remains on the cloth. The wafer must be trampled before...............

We are erected with the gates before us. We greet HIM with great exaltation. HE is with us again. My head is spinning, my hands damp from excitement. Cesar never knew such adoration and dedication. For if indeed we taste death tonight, we will have seen what others simply dream of and crave. SATAN is with us and to HIM we give the thanks and glory.

Book of Satanic Ritual

"Gloria in Excelsis Diaboli!!"
The chalice will soon be filled with the elixir of vigor and intense vitality. Drink with HIM and let all witness HIS awesome power and intensity. She is HIS and we the assembled black congregation. A wafer, a dash, a scream!!!! All pray………."Amen………Evil From Us Deliver……." !!! We are in unison.

She screams!!!! Fate is for cowards. This night will open her door widely and she will know us all. I bless the chalice and hold it to the inviting lips of the High Priestess. She gives thanks and kisses my lips deeply. Her hair is long flowing black. I have called her heart and soul with gentle refrain. She kneel and touches me……………she knows exactly how a touch can bring a crescendo of ecstasy to a wondrous, frenetic pageant of artistry. She takes me fully and I begin to accelerate in a steady ascent to the pinnacle perch of the sanctum. Chanting, chanting; "Bread Daily Our Day………." My head is spinning with sensitive, building passion amplifying with every smooth motion. I will soon reward her with the victuals of her labor. "Heaven In Art Who….." She is taking me to that sublime sphere where all is seen in slowness and in a unity we allow the deepest to emerge. Father is unaffected by the young gasp and screams as a wounded animal being devoured in pieces. Hail Satan!!!

I explode as she points me toward a Paten of wafers in her left hand. I discharge the full load onto the contents of the plate. Father yells as loud as thunder and withdraws. The wafers then absorb the claret of her inner thighs…..so young and tender, she shakes. Our Father, as emerald lightning, departs and to us………HIS blessing lingers. The Paten is thrown to the floor and trampled………….my legs are weak but I deliver the benediction. Our princess is assisted by our priestess to a sitting position. It is complete! She is now "Family" and she will always have someone looking out for her and the interests of our "Silent Order".

"Silentium est Aureum…………………"

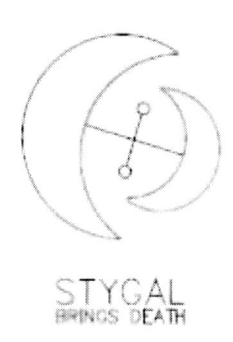

Exorcism and the Church

During ceaseless study and research for my books and books, I sometimes find an interesting point to further investigate in the search of Satanic enlightenment.

Rituale Romanum. The words themselves conjure thoughts of the Satanic, or at least the occult. Is this a sinister grimoire written by a coven or witches or a Magus performing a ritual of sacrifice?

Neither. The Rituale Romanum is actually a book of sacraments from none other than the Catholic Church. The book, originally written in Latin for those conducting "blessed and sanctioned" rituals from the church. The book covers several rituals including Baptism, Confirmation, Penance, Matrimony and Death. Chapter XIII is reserved for an interesting ritual; something most people would never associate with the Christian Church.....The Rite of Exorcism.

In the middle of a Priest's "how to book" we find an interesting subject that not only recognizes demonic possession but actually proceeds to explain the institutional foundation as a holy abutment; complete with step by step actions to assist the Priest with an effective and efficient exorcism of the demonic resident.

The reason I am going to great lengths to explain this in detail is simply a selfish motive. I have maintained that demons and Satan himself are real and tangible beings that have (and currently continue to) manifest themselves during our Satanic Rituals and ceremonies. I have met with "less that enthusiastic support" from others in the Satanic community in the past. Only those followers who have witnessed the happenings recorded in my books such as A Satanic Grimoire truly believe without some tongue in cheek roll of the eyes or contained chuckles. I admit, sometimes as I am confessing to such witnessed events, I often pause to ensure I am not going CRAZY but it is REAL. I have never lied nor embellished the events and I have recorded them exactly as they happened.

To add to my evidence of the existence of demonic beings, I submit the Rituale Romanum. To explore the artery of religious thought, let me begin by prefacing the following by stating: I am a believer of demons and Satan as anthropomorphic beings. Anything less would be a lie to myself and I will be true to my beliefs no matter what the rebuttal from the non believers.

My first point is quite simple and straightforward; If the church did not (or does not currently) believe in the physical manifestation of demons, why would they devote a chapter in their ceremonial "how to" book that is supposed to be interpreted exactly as written? The Rituale Romanum is not a book of philosophy nor is it a book of stark fiction. There is also the absence of arguments or hardline justifications for the rituals therein. The book does not ask those involved if they believe in matrimony, baptism or demonic possession; that fact is implied and accepted....no further discussions on the matter.

Frankly, the Rituale Romanum remains silent on the question of "does _____ exist" and it goes straight to the method to deal with the subject. Would the church open such a Pandora's box of questions and speculation if they did not unequivocally believe in the anthropomorphic beings also?

If you will notice, I use the word "currently" when asking about the church's belief. We have all witnessed the shifting sands of time that are forcing the established church to reassess their positions on many of today's issues and we have also witnessed the about-face of some stances the church has taken in the past. This being said, it would seem that if the church currently dismissed possession and the amalgamation of such claims, Section XIII would surely have been removed from the Rituale Romanumin keeping with the changing position. It has not been removed from the document and remains therein.

The Litanies of the Rituale Romanum also support the acceptance of demons as real and communicable beings; able to transfer from one human to another through a methodology that humans have not yet been able to positively identify, This reminds me of AIDS, when it first arrived on the scene in the 70s and 80s. Some of the same questions were raised without ample information, facts, data or knowledge, Could AIDS be spread through a handshake, toilet seat or it a person sneezed............would it infect everyone in the close proximity of the infected person? Everyone was grasping at answers.

In the Litanies, the same unknown is subliminally communicated to the reader: "Can the demon enter the priest, other in the room and / or "infect" them by touching, speaking to or other methods?" The core question being "Is evil contagious? Can a person "catch" evil?" If the church was and is so sure about the matters of the spirit, why would such a question even be presented in a handbook instead of some philosophical dissertation or treatise? The answer: The all-mighty church is unsure and cannot speak intelligently to the subject (Reference).

The Rite of Exorcism is not just sanctioned by the local parishes but certain section of the Rituale Romanum are figuratively redacted by the Vatican by including the following statement in the associated sections: "The texts of the Rite of Exorcism are restricted to the study and use of Exorcist Priests who perform this ministry under the direction of the Diocesan Bishop". In keeping with the Hocus Pocus line of thought and the conspiracy theorists' revelation, the church actually refuses to officially reduce the selected section to writing and thus, the priest must have a "fail-safe" type of mission briefing to properly prepare for waging cognitive warfare on the demons of the Satanic Pit.

In the last subtitle of Section XIII of the Rituale Romanum subsists "Exorcism of Satan and the Fallen Angels". Yes, there it is in black and white; the admittance of Satanic Possession, a fact I have known of and witnessed many times over my lifetime. The church not only admits the existence of this phenomena but also offers the checklist for dealing with "Good 'Ole Satan" himself.

This is the part where I must provide some tongue in cheek-contained chuckles. I have witnessed Satan in His awe, glory and power and I testify before Him that a few well-chosen words, a couple splashes of toilet water and a crucifix thrown in for good measure will not – I repeat

Book of Satanic Ritual

WILL NOT contain the Master of the World nor will it restrain Him any at all.

Satan and His demons are all-powerful. You cannot and will not contain that which is simply light years ahead of your humanistic understanding. As I have said before, we do not control demons or Satan; They control us. This is another reason I recognize novice "Satanic Gurus" immediately when reading their thoughts on this subject. You do not and will never be able to "command the forces of darkness" to appear, do your bidding or any other commandment. These beings are not trained animals............they do not perform tricks and if you approach magic from that misguided perspective, you will learn the meaning of being the "Devil's Wrath". I digress.

A Few Important Points

1. Satan is real. He is an anthropomorphic being that is capable of manifesting Himself as a physical presence.

2. Demons are real. They too can occupy physical

space in our world.

3. The established church knows Satan and Demons are real and can possess those humans of their choosing.

4. The church attempts to provide guidance to priests concerning possession and exorcism through the Rituale Romanum.

5. The church continues to believe in the powers of darkness and attempts (without success) to mitigate and control those powers.

6. Satan nor His Demons can be controlled, coerced nor commanded to do anything nor abstain from doing anything they desire. This "commanding" language used by some Satanists is evidence of their lack of understanding and Satanic knowledge. These individuals are treading dangerously close to a very "hard lesson to learn".

PS: *Rock of Ages, fall on thee*..........

Book of Satanic Ritual

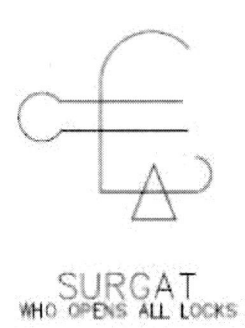

SURGAT
WHO OPENS ALL LOCKS

PART IV

I have been involved in the Satanic Black Arts for most of my life and that is why I have a very, very large extended family within the Satanic community. I do not use the word "family" lightly. I have a wonderful family that worships together and supports one another. While involved with the Christian church, I never felt as close to nor as comfortable as I do with my Satanic family. At the very core of this feeling is my local coven. I feel the nucleus of my family is the coven and all other involvement, whether with affiliated covens or the larger demographic, is adding value to the basic group.

All humans desire to belong in a group of like-minded individuals. We all have a deep need to be desired and loved. For me, the coven fulfills that yearning and makes me feel whole. There is also another wonderful advantage to belonging to a coven and getting to know the members intimately; the mental and sexual connection with the other demonic kindred spirits.

The need for sexual intercourse is a most powerful driving force in human nature; second only to food and water, so it is no surprise that people constantly think about, talk about, dream about and fantasize about Sex. The need to spread the seed or receive and nurture the very fluid that, when combined with the egg, can bring forth the possibility for another human being to be created is the very essence of continuing the human race. The very word "intercourse" stirs warm feelings in the erogenous areas of both man and woman; both aching and longing to satisfy the urges in orgasmic release. With the passing of time and the free exchange of sexual encounters in every corner of the world, it was only a matter of time before something would go terribly wrong.......enter AIDS.

As the epidemic swept across the globe, there were

those narrow-minded fools that believed AIDS was a homosexual disease and heterosexuals were immune to the spreading illness. It was during that critical period that many "heterosexuals" contracted the deadly illness due to their ignorance. In the current society, everyone knows unprotected sexual intercourse could possibly be a "death sentence"; literally. So what does all this have to do with the Satanic coven?

In today's sexual protected and tense world, the Satanic coven is an oasis in the desert of celibacy. Knowing the members of the group on such intimate terms is an advantage when dealing with the undeniable urge to "fuck". Yes, there are many possible "mutually beneficial" alliances that can be successfully cultivated and both (or more) members can have very rewarding experiences. This begins with penis and vagina but sometimes, the sharing of a few moments of passion lead to a much deeper connection and sometimes reveals the illusive "soul mate" link that so many people search for their entire lives.

Another of the benefits is the fact that neither person needs to feel uneasy, uncomfortable or embarrassed with their desires and / or preferences. In the coven (as in Satanism itself) there is no place for shame or feelings of fear concerning their sexuality. If both (or more) individuals are satisfied, "mission accomplished". Who wants to feel like they are being judged for secret desires they want fulfilled? Certainly, a Satanist will not have such feelings and / or apprehensions.

The Satanic coven can be much more than friends; the coven can be the strong social glue that holds the members together and allows them to fully realize their true potential as Satanists. Take the time to cultivate relationships in the coven and within other covens as well to expand your knowledge of our magic and to support one another while perhaps serving a much greater physical need.

Book of Satanic Ritual

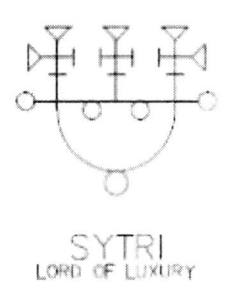

SYTRI
LORD OF LUXURY

An excerpt from an article by Andrew Crivilare

Signs of the Illuminati are supposedly everywhere. But according to an Eastern professor, the Illuminati have not existed in more than two centuries and have no plans on returning.

Gustavo Albear, an assistant professor of secondary education and foundations, was the speaker at "The History of the Illuminati" lecture. Albear said the Illuminati were indeed once an organization with motives toward removing religious influence in European government, but collapsed under political pressure prior to the French Revolution. "You're not going to be seeing one walking around anymore, they're gone," Albear said. "They're off the face of the earth."

Albear said that the first people to take the title of Illuminati were those baptized into Christianity, thus becoming "illuminated" with the knowledge of God. A group during the 18th century adopted the name Illuminati. They schemed to integrate themselves amongst the power brokers of Europe by aligning themselves with the charitable values of Freemasonry without informing people of their treasonous plot or the dangers involved, Albear said.

Today, the Illuminati are associated with Satanism and Devil worship, in part due to the influence of pop media such as Dan Brown's stories, Albear said. "I want you to understand the Illuminati are not Satanists," he said. "That's stuff Mr. Brown shoves in for giggles."

Albear said the Freemasons ties to the Illuminati more than 200 years ago continues to color public opinion on who the Masons are and their activities."

I regularly read numerous books to get a feel for the current thought and rationale of mainstream culture. Some posts are quite interesting and well thought out, which is very refreshing to read while some are simply a "line of bullshit" in the form of prose. There have been more and more of the "dark and brooding" posts lately and some are well done as high art and others are just plain belly aching and pointless bantering.

There are more suicidal books emerging around the world and to tell you the truth…………it gets old very quickly. The world sucks, they have been "wronged" and no gives a shit about anyone else……."Dry the tears and do something with yourself". Every person has something to offer society so log off and shut up!!

There are some people who will never be happy and that is an accepted fact. I do, however think some of these individuals would serve a higher calling if they would but stop feeling sorry for themselves. What you put into life is what you get out of it so if complaining is all that is put in there will be nothing but misery received. It is a vice that can be, at the end game, deadly in its conclusion. WAKE UP.

For the last two weeks I have followed this one young woman through this exact cycle. She is not

Book of Satanic Ritual

a beauty queen but she is pleasant and certainly not grotesque. She has attributes and simply down plays her ability to be more that she is……currently. I find it to be a tremendous waste of time, resources and ultimately her youth; which runs out so quickly.

She is adamant to "fish" for complements from her visitors. I have never commented nor spoken to her at all. I watch while either young boys or old scallywags toy with her words in certain sexual innuendos and tedious responses. She is as a puppy seeking approval of her "guests" while deeply craving something more. She wants to leave the town she lives in; she wants to start over; she posts pics of her friends from long ago in some unattainable effort to resurrect the "good old days" of her past. She posts pics of couples having intercourse and acts of fellatio and cunnilingus while commenting a sigh or emoticons.

I have seen many girls who found Satanism after floundering in the same unproductive cycle and they became stable, happy and satisfied individuals; physically and spiritually as well. I have vowed to remain silent but perhaps finding Satan would have the same impact and break the chain that will one day figuratively (and realistically) strangle the life out of her.

Satan and the Satanic followers throughout the world recognize a person has strengths and there are possibilities that can be released with only the exchange of words. If the "world" does not want or need these individuals, Satanism will gladly receive them with open arms. As a Magus, I envision a person's capabilities and look beyond the "face value" to find the strength that can be tangibly realized by that person if they will only stop crying and begin trying. There is always room at the Satanic feast and Satan wants you!!!

When working Satanic Magic spells, be sure to clear your mind of everything except for the focus of the working. When you are having trouble concentrating, you should stop the ritual work and meditate for a few minutes or until you can control your thoughts. This is a very crucial part of magic overall but it especially applies to spells. The focus of your energy must be precise; it should be honed to a Laser point that you are always in control of and are continuously increasing the potency of the energy being generated. Anything less will fail to yield the desired outcome and will perhaps, harm you as a byproduct instead.

Many people overlook meditation in their daily lives and that is a real shame. There are so many benefits from frequent meditation and clearing of the mind, chakras and channels. Among the benefits is the repair of the brain through calming introspection and rumination. This maintenance and repair is needed to ensure the magic and spirit remain firmly connected; for without one, there can not exist the other.

Before your next magical working, invite those with you to meditate with you. Formulate the way you (as a group or alone) visualize the outcome of the magical working that will soon follow. When the group agrees upon one unanimous image in the mind's eye, begin the meditation process. This may seem a waste of time for those new to magic so your group must be willing to explain and teach the benefits of such an investment of time. I am confident your workings will yield much greater, successful outcomes. Stress the importance of such an endeavor and make it part of future practices.

Book of Satanic Ritual

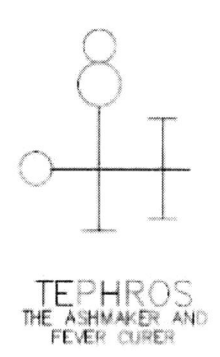

TEPHROS
THE ASHMAKER AND
FEVER CURER

Benedict XVI Won't Go There

Father Gabriele Amorth works in the dark. But also by the light of day, this faithful priest says his job is often at odds with the rest of the Catholic Church. He became the official exorcist of diocese of Rome in June 1986, during John Paul II's papacy. Today, at 86, this member of Society of St. Paul is still fighting what he calls "the Great Enemy." The devil is his name.

Father Amorth tells the story of his lifelong battle against Satan in the newly published book "L'Ultimo Esorcista" (The Last Exorcist). The book was written together with Paolo Rodari, a

journalist with the Italian newspaper Il Foglio.
Besides Lucifer, the priest's other enemies are all those people who don't believe the devil exists.
"Your Eminence, you should read a book," father Amorth once told a powerful cardinal of the Roman Curia who had said the devil was just "a result of superstition."
The cardinal asked: "What book?"
"The Gospels," Amorth shot back. "Am I wrong or are the exorcisms one of Jesus's primary activities?"
The priest practices eight to 10 exorcisms a day, including on Sunday and Christmas day. He thinks the devil is everywhere, even in the Vatican's holy rooms. He says that John Paul II was convinced as well, and also practiced his own exorcisms.
The Polish pontiff's first exorcism took place on March 27, 1982. The then bishop of the central Italy town of Spoleto, Ottorino Alberti, brought a young woman, Francesca Fabrizi, to him. Once in front of him, she started to sob, writhing on the ground, despite the Pope's commands for the devil to retreat. She calmed down only when John Paul II said: "Tomorrow I will say mass for you."
A few years later, the woman visited John Paul

together with her husband. She was peaceful, happy, and pregnant. "I've never seen anything like this before," the Pope told the head of the papal household, Cardinal Jacques Martin, according to the latter's memoirs. "It was a biblical scene," the Pope added.

Current Pope Benedict XVI does not perform exorcisms, but Amorth believes the devil considers him even more dangerous than John Paul II. In his book, Amorth writes that two of his assistants took two victims of demonic possession to St. Peter's Square to see a papal general audience. When they saw the Pope, they fell to the ground, rolling around, screaming and drooling. Benedict noticed them, got closer, and blessed them. It looked like they had been lashed, and knocked backwards severa meters. Amorth writes.

According to Amorth, the devil has always tempted the Church hierarchies and the inhabitants of the Vatican. He says that Satanic sects are behind the case of Emanuela Orlandi, the daughter of a Vatican City employee who mysteriously disappeared on June 22, 1983.

"A 15-year-old girl [as Orlandi was at the time]

does not get it in a car if she does not know the person inviting her to get in. I think investigations were necessary inside, not outside the Vatican. I think that only someone that Emanuela knew well could have convinced her to get in the car. Often Satanic sects do it: they invite a girl in a car and then they make her disappear."

In 1999, Luigi Marinelli, a retired priest and a former member of the Vatican's Congregation for Eastern Churches, published the book "Gone with the Wind In The Vatican" denouncing nepotism, corruption, and sexual scandals of the Catholic Church. But no one did anything. "It should have been an alarm bell for the Church. But it wasn't," says Amorth.

The priest believes that the devil tempts everyone: religious and lay people, adults and children. A striking case happened in the small northern Italian town of Chiavenna in June 2000, when three teenagers killed a nun named Maria Laura Mainetti. They later said it was a sacrifice to the devil. At the time, the press put the emphasis on the girls' obsession for esotericism and worship of the rock singer Marilyn Manson.

"Of course, I cannot say the cause of the murder

was Manson's song or Manson himself," says Amorth. "But let's be clear: Satanic music is one of the main vehicles to spread Satanism among young people. The messages of Satanic music influence the hearts and minds of young people. Via this kind of music, young people get in touch with new and previously unknown topics. They reach evil's frontiers, places they had not explored before."

Book of Satanic Ritual

Book of Satanic Ritual

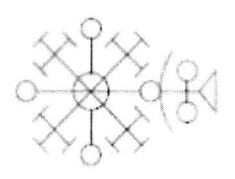

VALAC
LORD OF SNAKES

Satanic energy is needed for working of magical spells, curses, rituals, rites, etc. Learning to harness this energy is a challenge for the beginner new to the Left Hand Path. There is one thing more challenging to the beginner; finding the Satanic energy.
"Where does it come from and what can you do with it?" You begin the journey............
Satan has made many of the mysteries of the past known and there are many good books and lessons on the subject. There is almost a "sensory overload" of Satanic information out in the cyber world. How do you know you are doing it the right way? How can you protect yourself from

Book of Satanic Ritual

harm when working with the energy? Is there a source to absorb and learn the many different aspects of magic? Who has the right formula for making the magic work?

So many questions and so few answers for the beginner. This is frustrating and often leads to the beginner simply giving up on the truth in exchange for fabricated lies of some "cult guru". After wasting time, money and energy on a path leading to a dead end, the beginner goes on the next thing he / she heard or read about................never truly knowing if Satanism was their answer and their life path. It is an overwhelming waste of epic proportion.

I have noticed some people searching..............one week they are into "Hail Satan" and the following week they are speaking of the Cone of Power. Experimentation is fine but it should never define who the person is and wants to be. A person "searching and experimenting" should not loose sight of who they truly are.

The point is no one should loose themselves to the point of imitation when it comes to one's beliefs. We see this happen in style and fashion everyday; white kids imitating a *gangsta* rapper.

Book of Satanic Ritual

Flattery is the truest form of complement but Satan does not want imitations...............He wants the REAL THING.

Those who will learn, experiment and always strive to become more powerful through the acquisition of knowledge. He does not want a fraud..........leave that for the Christians. He wants a pure heart and motivation with which He can mold and make a true Satanic Warrior.

Simply put: "He wants those willing to be the trend setter instead of the trend follower".

Set your course and keep your mind open. Satan wants you to succeed and He will show you the way.

Dedicated to the Master of the World......Lord Satan.

Book of Satanic Ritual

VEGUANIEL
ARCHDEMON OF FORTUNE

Satanic Beauty

Each week, I receive over one hundred emails from those who have stumbled upon my book. Some are writing to ask questions concerning the authenticity of Satanism as a life – changing event and some are really searching for answers along their spiritual journey. I also receive scathing email from those who call themselves Christians. They chastise, beg, barter, present bible babble and even resort to cursing me (yes profanity from the lips of the chosen ones) because I simply refuse to bow to their peer pressure and psychological warfare. There are very few people I actually invest the energy needed to hate them but these idiots – I truly HATE………at least for a few minutes anyway.

Often, I receive multiple correspondence from searchers and I always answer their emails and try to address their concerns and questions. As a result, I have actually formed a repore with some of them and I enjoy discussing all things Satanic with them. Humans are social creatures and as such, I derive a great deal of pleasure from spirited volleys of differing topics.

I also have those Satanic Groupies (so to speak) that enjoy sending me pornographic pictures of themselves in certain Evil Noir poses……and I greatly enjoy lusting as I open the pics with morbid curiosity and delight. Women are such wonderful creatures and I take such pleasure in looking at their beautiful bodies………….true Satanic Beauty!!

I have a metaphorical "soft spot" in my heart for those truly searching and seeking spiritual truth. I guess this originates from seeing myself in their bantering, fumbling and overwhelming excitement as they discover Satanism and true magic. Many years I had to conform to the dictates of the established church and far too long did I endure the pain and emptiness of the church. Too many friends lost in the blinding "white light" of the congregation; under a microscope, every word measured, every motivation questioned, an open book to a world full of self – righteous, self ordained and self – worshiping theological rapists; symbolically sodomizing anyone who would question their doctrine.

I find the majority of my time is spent guiding and counseling our Covens. I have enjoyed being in a position that make people comfortable discussing their innermost feelings, concerns and thoughts. Our groups are closely tied and I often attend other workings so I too can receive something new; something fresh and something exciting. This does not mean I do not receive those things from my coven – it simply means I enjoy new experiences too. We are all searchers and we will always seek something that will renew our inner spirit.

Following the LHP is more than rituals, magic and fulfilling the carnal urges and primal proclivities. Satanism is about discovery, knowledge, willpower, emotions, understanding and a deep concern for the SELF. Without a healthy SELF, there is no hope of happiness, satisfaction or self discovery.

Just as clearing the Chakras is important for health, clearing the mind of unwanted "baggage" is a necessity. You will experience the greatest awakening when you begin treating YOURSELF as the most important GOD. Without this "key" you cannot open the locks that chain you to the lies of religion. Stop running, compose yourself and say "NO MORE"!!

Open your inner self to the answers and begin learning and stop lying to yourself. Established religion has nothing to offer you; but Satanism can give you the world. You are not alone………..ever. We are with you, the Demons are with you and our loving Master Satan is with you. He is willing and able to show you a world you cannot even fathom. He will guide you through the darkness of rhetoric and lies that the church has sold throughout history to those poor, dying souls. You deserve more and you can have more. You can have something real and tangible.

Book of Satanic Ritual

Satan calls………..will you answer?

Write me and let me know you have started your journey of truth. I would love to hear from you.

And ladies, feel free to send me some pics……….you know the ones I like!!!

Book of Satanic Ritual

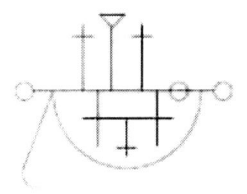

VEPAR
THE WATER MASTER

"In nomine Magni Dei Nostri Satanas. Hail Satan!"

"The Sacred Symbols – the Horns of Power, the Egg of Purity, Safety and Life, etc., exist in the most terrifying appearances. Everything that is, is holy."

Aleister Crowley

Liber Oz
There is no god but Man. Man has the right to live by his own law –
to live in the way that he wills to do:
to work as he will:

to play as he will:
to rest as he will.
to die when and how he will:
Man has the right to eat what he will:
to drink what he will:
to dwell where he will:
to move as he will on the face of the earth.
Man has the right to think what he will:
to speak what he will:
to write what he will:
to draw, paint, carve, etch, mould, build as he will:
to dress as he will.
Man has the right to love as he will: —
"take your fill and will of love as ye will,
when, where and with whom ye will!" — AL. I. 51.
Man has the right to resist those who would thwart these rights.
"the slaves shall serve." — AL. II. 58.

Aleister Crowley has been identified with the occult for many years (Golden Dawn). His writings are quoted by many followers of Satanism, Black Magick and the Occult. Crowley's thoughts and observations are almost synonymous with the "extremity" of dabbling in the search for the inescapable Will of man.

"I slept with Faith, and found a corpse in my arms on awaking; I drank and danced all night with Doubt, and found her a virgin in the morning."

Aleister Crowley - "Book of Lies"

The Abbey of Thelema refers to a small house which was used as a temple and spiritual center founded by Aleister Crowley and Leah Hirsig in Cefalù, Sicily in 1920. The name remains a popular name for various magical societies, Witchcraft covens, and Satanic Grottoes. While in a relative state of disrepair, the structure still stands.
While some worship Crowley himself, others see him as a visionary – an Iconoclast of the Left Hand Path. Few can argue Crowley pushed the limits of magic and humanistic indulgence to a new frontier through his constant searching and experimentation in all things Human. Without reservation, Crowley never limited himself to preconceived boundaries and he exposed the world of freedom that very few have or ever will experience. During his life, his followers would

come and go however he would never stray far from symbolically "dancing on the razor blade" and it exposed those followers to what some would call inexplicable acts of mistreatment, mental / physical depravity, torture and sexual degradation. No can deny he was open to any forces of the universe that would come his way. There are those who have tried in vain to replicate his experiments. It can be said that flattery is the highest form of compliment but it is just that: replication.

Crowley (aka The Great Beast) experimented extensively with sex magick; escaping the sexual limitations and taboos of the times. His motivation was to experience anything that would broadening his horizons, knowledge and relentlessly seeking enlightenment. The Order of the Temple of the East, or the Order of Oriental Templar is an international fraternal and religious organization founded at the beginning of the 20th century.

English author and occultist Aleister Crowley has become the most well known member of the order. Originally it was intended to be modeled after and associated with Freemasonry, but under the leadership of Aleister Crowley, O.T.O. was reorganized around the Law of Thelema as its central religious principle. This Law—expressed as "Do what thou Wilt shall be the whole of the Law" and "Love is the law, love under will"—was promulgated in 1904 with the dictation of The Book of the Law.

Crowley was extremely intelligent and he often used this to his advantage through "tongue and cheek" patronizing comments. Author and Crowley expert Lon Milo Duquette wrote in his 1993 work The Magick of Aleister Crowley:

"Crowley clothed many of his teachings in the thin veil of sensational titillation. By doing so he assured himself that one, his works would only be appreciated by the few individuals capable of doing so, and two, his works would continue to generate interest and be published by and for the benefit of both his admirers and his enemies long after death. He did not—I repeat not—perform or advocate human sacrifice. He was often guilty, however, of the crime of poor judgment. Like all of us, Crowley had many flaws and shortcomings. The greatest of those, in my opinion, was his inability to understand that everyone else in the

world was not as educated and clever as he. It is clear, even in his earliest works, he often took fiendish delight in terrifying those who were either too lazy, too bigoted, or too slow-witted to understand him."

Book of Satanic Ritual

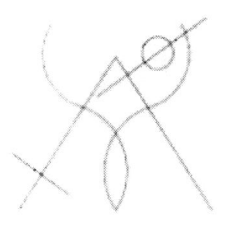

VETIS
THE LIFE PROMISER

Outliving Usefulness

As a Satanist, I have very few *substantial* fears. I am not afraid of the usual things others fear...........death, the Devil, the dark, etc. I do not hide in the crowd trying to become invisible. I like confrontation and I am not afraid of doing "what needs to be done" for the betterment of those who deserve better. I suppose of all the things I could fear, I am without that limiting emotional rock around my neck.

One thing I do fear is outliving my usefulness. While Satan has assured me that will be sometime in the distant future (since I continue to do His work, not my work) I do face that inevitable time with angst. Satan is not a Filicide. However, who wants to be around when no one wants them around or when their ideas and opinions no longer hold validity or are accepted as a well-made point?

With the advances in medicine, we are living longer lives. Our bodies have been preserved and preventive measures used to ensure the holistic health however, more often the physical body remains stronger than the mental health. For this reason, we as society are facing more elderly that are "fit as a fiddle"......except for the all-important mind. These individuals are often "warehoused" in convalescence homes or other hospice facilities where they simply wait to die. Some say the solution is population control while others advocate laws that would protect the rights for such individuals to end their lives on their terms through assisted suicide.

Let's face it, some people and institutions often outlive their usefulness to society as a whole. Religion is one such organization and it is time to ask "Has religion outlived its usefulness?" Since the beginning of time, humans has sought was to control one another and religion has been at the forefront in this endeavor. More blood has been spilled over religion than any other subject in existence. Why should it continue to be allowed to exist, since everyone knows the true motivations of their "flocks"? Why not snuff out religion completely; after all it has far outlived its hyperbole fabrication and as for usefulness…………..useful only to those wishing to in prison those free thinkers and rationalists.

If these evangelical criminals were removed from the throne of power and those intelligent people who know the church for what it truly is (big business that sells fake forgiveness for being human) spoke up and took the power and authority, the world would be a better place. The church is a club and a business. Being human does not require a blessing, forgiveness or a payment plan………….how long will the insanity continue?

Excommunication from the church is sometimes the only thing that saves people. Certainly, in a rational world, rational thought should overcome suspicion, lies, superstition and nonexistent proof.

Book of Satanic Ritual

Since the beginning of recorded history, religion has symbolically crucified the average person and forced them to run in circles, jump through hoops and bow to empty statues in order to "fit" into the peer pressure-driven congregations of dying religions. Each generation is fooled into believing they must "measure up" to some fictitious standard and cease being human. Meanwhile, the liars have their hands in the man's wallet and up the woman's dress; filling their own greed-driven lusts and desires all the while hiding behind a veneer of sacred and holiness………….in touch with their so-called god.

Reductio ad Absurdum

Evil takes many forms and one of the easiest for the shyster is the illusion of an all-knowing, all-seeing and benevolent leader of the pack. What a farce and a great lie. There is only the law of survival and religion has ensured their survival by killing anyone who has ever dared to question the ludicrous and outlandishness of their guide book…………..a collection of foolish banter bound together in leather called the bible.

So who are the bigger fools? Is it those who sell such old, tired and useless lies or the ones who gobble it up like some fine cuisine? If people turned and walked away from the lies of religion, the leaders would soon find themselves without followers, without an audience and most importantly, without income. Without the lure of money, most of these con men (and women) would soon find their control over the populous evaporated.

Religion is old, tired and has lost its cognitive abilities. It is time to rise up and speak the truth...............Religion should be put to death. It is a brave new world and the future has countless possibilities.

If religion and the established church have a place in the future, it is because we (as society) have allowed it to live on............well past its usefulness!!!!

Book of Satanic Ritual

Book of Satanic Ritual

ZABLAH
OF HELL'S ELECTORATE
"LAWYER"

Anton LaVey

I have followed several conversations on "Satanic" websites that revolve around the denial of Satan as an anthropomorphic being. I have been urged by coven members to chime in on the subject and so, I will indulge in some philosophical pontificating.

In approaching a sensitive subject as this, I will take the liberty of speaking my mind; as my beliefs are somewhat based upon experiences instead of *"what someone else claims to be the facts"*.

Those who have not read my books often ask me

what type of Satanism our covens practice. Usually, the question also makes reference to Anton LaVey and do I practice his "Type of Satanism".

First, for those who have never researched Anton, he was not a Satanist in the truest sense. Anton and his group were more "Atheist" that "Satanist". I do find his writings to be accurate on some points; especially when it comes to the hypocritical "church" but on the serious subject of Satanism, he missed the mark.

For example, his writings concerning the "anthropomorphic Satan" are geared for the atheist and not the Satanist. He spoke in this topic in many of his interviews; saying "…..if a person wants to believe in a "real" Satan, it is fine with us. If the person needs to believe in the being, it is his / her prerogative."

So here is one of the founding fathers of Satanism actually denying the existence of Satan. I have some heartburn over that. While conformance is not the objective, believing in Satan is almost a "***prerequisite***" to becoming a Satanist………in my humble opinion.

I do respect Anton's works, writings and he did

further the cause of Satanism. I also find many of his quotes to be accurate and quite refreshing as he spoke his mind on the psychology of human beings. He was straightforward in his approach and took a lot of criticism and chastisement from the Christian "Neanderthal" Church. It is not always easy to be the point of verbal attacks and mockery repeatedly. For that, I have the utmost respect for him.

"Most Satanists do not accept Satan as an anthropomorphic being with cloven hooves, a barbed tail, and horns. He merely represents a force in nature – the powers of darkness which have been named just that because no religion has taken these forces out of the darkness. Nor has science been able to apply technical terminology to this force. It is an untapped reservoir that few can make use of because they lack the ability use a tool without having to first break down and label all the parts which make it run. It is this incessant need to analyze which prohibits most people from taking advantage of this many faceted key to the unknown – which the Satanist chooses to call "Satan". Satan, as a god, demi-god, personal

savior, or whatever you wish to call him, was invented by the formulators of every religion on the face of the earth for only one purpose – to preside over man's so-called wicked activities and situations here on earth. Consequently, anything resulting in physical or mental gratification was defined as "evil" – thus assuring a lifetime of unwarranted guilt for everyone!"

The Satanic Bible

This passage clearly defines Anton's unbelief of Satan as an actual being. He simply leaves it up to the practitioner to decide if they believe in Satan or not. This is where my belief and Anton's belief diverge.

We believe in Satan because we have had occasion to be liberally blessed by His presence at magical workings and ceremonies. Satan is real and we have experienced Him in true form. Demons are also real and many have graced ceremonies I have attended over the years. You need not wonder if they truly exist, they do.

In my practice of the dark arts, I have experienced many events that simply defy explanation. Some would dismiss these happenings as parlor tricks performed by sleight of hand and others would simply never speak of the events ever again. I know there are always skeptics and those who would not truly believe if Satan stood in front of them in person. Does Satan truly exist…………..the answer is yes.

Therefore, if these posers do not believe in Satan, their magic is, in actuality, rendered fruitless and inept. Their coven is reduced to farcical fantasy role-play social faction and the followers are babbling meaningless prose in vain.

Mastema has greatly blessed our covens and the rich rewards for respect, worship and invitations to share the vast knowledge He has is wonderful. Without His guidance, we would simply be reciting empty recitations and performing dead rituals. This is the point I have tried to make so many times before to those wanting "drive through" Satanism. It will not and does not work! The words on a page are empty; the Inner Sanctum is void and the coven is a social club without the guidance and attendance by Satan and His host of Hellish Demons.

It is the evolution of magic and the giant leap of

faith, backed up with actions, that takes the practitioner's magic to new heights. Without this crucial element, your ceremonies will always be devoid of desired results. Every member of the coven MUST be in tune and faithful in seeking the maximum magical reward. Satan is willing (and more that able) to deliver but you must be willing and able to receive, learn, apply and exercise extreme dedication in order to benefit. Since I have discussed the benefits of Satan's blessings during your rituals, let us also discuss the repercussions of not inviting Satan and His Demons to a Satanic Ritual.

Without truly believing and respecting Satan's reality and certainty, the practitioner is symbolically "thumbing their nose at the entire underworld of Hell". Mockery is not acceptable behavior for the Satanic and Mastema will not allow it to continue without redress. By doing so, the practitioner is playing with Satanic fire and will be burned. Enough said on this matter.

Satan is real; Demons are real; magic is real. If they play with fire while giving no recognition to its power, they will be consumed by that power. They are magically challenged imbeciles and knuckle-dragging buffoons.

Magical spells and rituals are administered and moderated by the Magus but the real power is from the Demonic Toastmaster himself, Satan. Rejuvenate the magic by inviting the true Master of Ceremony. Do not claim to be a Satanist if you are ordinary Atheist.

Book of Satanic Ritual

Book of Satanic Ritual

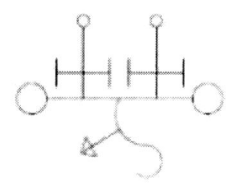

ZAGAM
LORD OF FORGERY

Satanists Do Not "Limit"

Life is short, time is an enemy and happiness is fleeting for those lucky enough to have found it. There is one thing you can do to in your pursuit of happiness…………be truthful with yourself.
Any religion will set boundaries and limitations on you but for the Satanist, we do not "limit" nor do we judge.
If you are seeking happiness, ring in the new year with truthfulness, explore the spiritual world around you and stop carrying guilt, shame and pain.
TRUTH………give it as try.
In the role of Satanic Magus, I often have

followers of the LHP confide in me and seek my advice. I willingly assist whenever possible, as my mission is to further the cause of Satanism worldwide. I especially enjoy helping those "searchers" who know there is something more out there than the dictates of the established church or other "slave / master" arrangements.

As with anything new, the searchers are apprehensive, suspicious and uncertain as to what Satanism is all about and especially the motives of our groups. More than this, the searcher is looking to fill that void in their heart and soul that desperately needs to be satiated. When a searcher takes that all-important first step, it is a step of faith: they are saying "I know there is more out there and I want more!"

I have expressed my opinions of women in several posts and in my books as well. There are however, times I feel so inclined to say much more and I suppose this is one of those times.

I believe women have been slighted in the realm of theology. Women have much to contribute to any discussion on "religion" and for those who have truly seen the benefits of Satanism, they offer even more pellucid points. Women are intelligent and not to circumvent the issue, women are beautiful and worshipful creatures.

From the beginning of recorded history, women have been somewhat brushed to the side of all religions and are usually sequestered in the family home to rear the children, cook, clean and service the man of the house (whenever and however he desires and demands). History has also been rewritten to ensure the chauvinistic agenda remains strong. One of the first beauties to be historically wronged is Lilith.

Lilith originated from Jewish mythology and story-telling. The Jews were the first to "spin" the story and establish Lilith as being evil. As the story goes, Lilith was forced by three angels (Sanvi, Sansanvi and Semangelaf) to swear she would not harm women or children wearing amulets bearing the angels' names.

Later, this story morphed into a belief that Adam and Lilith were actually husband and wife. After having sex with the archangel Samael outside the Garden of Eden, Lilith refused to submit to Adam's wishes any longer. She firmly refused to be obedient and subservient to Adam, which reached the pinnacle of the crescendo when Lilith demanded to be "on top" during sexual intercourse. This strong woman left Eden and married Samael. As the story goes, God (who the catholic church claims condemns the use of birth control of any kind) castrated Samael so the two could not procreate (go forth and multiply). There are several symbolic metaphors and contradictions in that one sentence.

OK, I digress. This is not a book on Lilith. It is about women and how they have received (and continue to receive) injustice from self-professed religious gurus who would rather have a women cleaning the church toilet than providing input on intellectual topics of discussion. In my opinion, Satanism will take any of the women rejected by or formally enslaved by established religions. Their loss is our gain. Religion continues to dominate women and subject them to such appalling actions as sexual mutilation, rape and degradation. You would think that in modern society, these outlandish, farcical and demeaning Neanderthals would have evolved into males who see women as they should be seen: intelligent and articulate beings.

As to the matter of sexuality, I believe women

should experiment and find what the right "thing" is for them personally. As I have sad before, Satanism does not wish to enslave anyone; quite the opposite! Satanism strives to unlock the door of inhibition and allow the person to explore and find what is right for them. Satanists do not need (or want) anyone to tell them what to believe or how to conduct themselves. Freedom of spirit, mind and body is the ultimate reward for the Satanist.

For the Satanic women reading this, I dedicate it to you and your uninhibited life and beautiful Satanic bodies!!

Do what Thou will shall be the whole of the law!!!!!!!!!!

Hail Satan

Book of Satanic Ritual

Book of Satanic Ritual

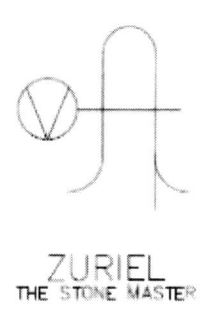

ZURIEL
THE STONE MASTER

Belial means "without a master," and symbolizes true independence, self-sufficiency, and personal accomplishment. Belial represents the earth element, and herein will be found magic with both feet on the ground—real, hard-core, magical procedure—not mystical platitudes devoid of objective reason. Probe no longer. Here is bedrock!

The Satanic Bible, The Book of Belial
Anton Szandor LaVey

Satanic magic is the use of magical forces or energies to enhance the life of an individual or individuals according to their desires. This usage can be of two types - the first is 'external' and the second is 'internal'. External magic is essentially sorcery: the changing of external events, circumstances or individuals in accordance with the wishes of the sorcerer. Internal magic is the changing of the consciousness of the individual magician using certain magical techniques -this is essentially the quest of the Initiate for the higher grades of magical attainment.

Ceremonial rituals are rituals involving more than two individuals, the ritual taking place in either a Temple or an outdoor area consecrated as a Temple. Ceremonial rituals involve a set text which is followed by the participants, and the wearing of ceremonial robes together with the use of certain items having magical or Occult significance. Hermetic rituals are usually undertaken by an individual working alone or with one assistant/ companion. To external magic belongs ceremonial and hermetic rituals. To internal magic belongs the seven-fold sinister way.

Satanists believe that we are already gods: but most people fail to understand this and continue

Book of Satanic Ritual

to grovel: to others or to a 'god'. Satanism, in its beginnings, is all about making conscious (or liberating) our dark or shadow nature, and to this end, Satanic magic is undertaken. Satanism is a natural expression of the evolutionary or *Promethean* urge within us: and its magic is a means to make us gods upon Earth, to realize the potential that lies within us all.

In traditional Satanism there is an appreciation of the role of women, for Satanism at its highest level is concerned with the development of the individual: roles as such are a necessary part of self-development. To be played, discarded and then transcended. The structure of traditional Temples and the rituals performed by those members of those Temples reflect this appreciation and understanding. For example, it is possible and indeed desirable for a Mistress of Earth to establish and organize her own Temple unless she herself wishes otherwise, just as it is possible and desirable to celebrate the Black Mass using a priest, naked, upon the altar while the Priestess conducts the service, such reversal being an accepted principle of Black Magic.

Satanic ceremonies are a means to enjoy the

pleasures of life: they offer carnality, the pleasure of fulfilling one's desires, the bringing of material and personal rewards and the joys of darkness. But they are only a beginning, a stage toward something greater.

Satanic rites are conducted either in an indoor Temple or in an isolated outdoor locality during the hours of darkness. Indoor Temples usually have a static altar, made of either stone or wood, and this altar should be set in the East. It should be covered by an altar cloth made of good quality material and colored black.

Upon this is woven either an inverted pentagram, the sigil or the personal sigil of the Master/Mistress or Temple if there is one. Candle-holders, made of either silver or gold, are placed on the altar, one at either end. Black candles are usually the most employed although some rituals require the use of other colors.

Other candleholders should be placed around the Temple, since the only light used in the Temple both during rituals and at other times should come from candles. The Black Book should be placed on an oak stand on the altar, the altar itself being of sufficient size for an individual to lie upon it.

Indoor Temples should be painted either black or crimson (or a combination of the two), the floor bare or covered with rugs or carpets of plain design, either black or crimson. When not in use, the Temple should be kept dark and warm, hazel incense being burned frequently. A quartz sphere or large crystal should be kept in the Temple, either in or near the altar: if near, supported by an oak stand.

Above the altar or behind it should be an image or sculpture of Baphomet according to Satanic Tradition. Baphomet is regarded by Satanists as a 'violent goddess' and is depicted as a beautiful woman, seated, who is naked from the waist up. In her left hand she holds the severed head of a man. In her other hand she holds a burning torch. The severed head, which drips blood onto her lower white garment, is held so that it partially obscures her smiling face. Baphomet is regarded as the archetype of the Mistress of Earth, and the Bride of Lucifer.

No other furnishings are present in the Temple. The Temple implements are few in number and should be either made or commissioned by the

Book of Satanic Ritual

Master or Mistress. If this is not possible, they should be chosen by them with care. The implements required are several large silver chalices, a Censor (or incense holders), a quartz tetrahedron, a large silver bowl, and the Sacrificial Knife which should have a wooden handle.

No one is allowed into the Temple unless they are dressed in ceremonial robes and barefoot. The robes are generally black with a hood, although some rituals require the use of other colors. If possible, an antechamber should be used by members to change into the ceremonial robes.

If an outdoor location is used, the area should be marked out by a circle of seven stones, by the Master or Mistress. An outdoor altar is usually the body of one of the participants - naked or robed depending on the ritual and the prevailing conditions. The one chosen for this honor lies on an altar cloth, black in color and woven with an inverted pentagram, the size of this cloth being not less than seven feet by three.

Candles should be placed in lanterns which open on one side only, this side being of glass which is often colored red. The participants should know the area well, since they should not use any artificial light of any kind including candles, to guide them to the chosen site. Neither must any fires be lit during any ritual. For this reason the night of the full moon is often chosen.

It is the duty of the Master and Mistress to prepare the members for the ritual. This usually involves them assembling in robes in the Temple or in an ante-chamber designated as a preparation area at least half of one hour before the beginning of the ritual. During this period they are to keep their silence while standing, concentrating on the image of Baphomet or some sigil (such as an inverted pentagram) as decreed by the Master or Mistress. One or several members should be chosen to act as Cantor and instructed in the proper chanting of the chants. Other members may be chosen as musicians - the preferred instruments being tabor (or hand-drum) or flute.

In considering the nature of any God, one must first consider the nature of man and of the universe, for without understanding himself or the universe in which he lives how can man approach an understanding of God? Each man possesses a consciousness independent of any other creature. He is aware of a separation between himself and the world around him. He experiences images, sounds, scents, tastes, and physical forms through what he perceives as his physical body. He also experiences thoughts, emotions, and other phenomena which do not manifest either visibly or audibly but which influence him nonetheless and which he perceives as coming from "within" his consciousness.

From the earliest times, man has attempted to reconcile this condition of "separation from the universe". Early man, in terror of the images and sounds which bombarded him from all directions and of the earth which seemed ready to swallow him once more as if the universe itself realized that it had made a terrible mistake, scared of this thing called "life" and yet equally scared of death, began to imagine hideous gods and demons all about him. These monsters which roared with anger and surely had the power to destroy him would have to be appeased or else death could be imminent.

Many people today have rejected the established religions of the past. This is natural when you consider that, while society has changed, the teachings and doctrines of these religions have not changed in over a thousand years. Many cannot reconcile the values and beliefs of society with the values and beliefs of the dominant religions within society. We are at a point in history where the dominant religions of the past will be displaced by religions whose values are in greater accordance with society's values today. This is why many people have sought out new religions and have turned to Wicca and new age philosophies or to alternative religious cults such as Heaven's Gate and the Solar Temple.

While cults devoted to new age mysticism or white light magic and spirituality have had some success among those seeking for "something or *anything* spiritual", due principally to Christianity's impoverishment of the ego and starvation of the intellect, they are ultimately no more relevant to today's society than the religions of the past.

The world is searching for a religion which embraces the scientific knowledge of today, recognizes the psychological nature of man, and perceives the potential of man to achieve far more than he has already, while holding to ethical beliefs and values held by society today, and possessing a willingness to change those values and beliefs in accordance with future changes in society. Despite some individuals who see in Satanism nothing more than anti-Christianity, a depraved religion of blasphemy or an expression for anti-social desires and impulses, the emphasis of Satanism on the ego and the intellect and its recognition of man's ultimate potential has made it the one religion relevant in today's society.

There is one thing common to all gods man has created. Every man-made god is static and unchanging. Yahweh resides in heaven, unchanging, unbending, the creator of the universe and all that it contains. Christ sits at the right hand of God ready to judge the living and the dead. Zeus resides in Mount Olympus holding aloft the lightning bolt, his symbol of divine power. The values of society and the structure of its institutions are defined as "good." That which threatens society is defined as "evil." The definitions of good or evil change from nation to nation and from century to century. God is defined by that which is "static" and unchanging. That which is "dynamic", a potential threat to the status-quo such as war, revolution, political unrest, or social upheaval, is represented by the Devil. But, if the universe is dynamic not static and consciousness is NOT but is becoming then the devil, Satan, more accurately reflects the true nature of God than Christ, Yahweh, or any other image of God which man creates and defines.

To the true sorcerer there is no "good" and no "evil"; there is only his *WILL*. This is the basis of Crowley's *Law of Thelema*. Those who interpret Crowley's law "do what thou WILL" as "do what you want" fail to understand that it is the magical WILL Crowley is referring to. What the sorcerer desires (or thinks that he desires) may not be the thing which his "higher self" has truly WILLED to occur.

Expanding upon the Law of Thelema, Michael Aquino conceptualized and proclaimed the Word *XEPER*, by which the sorcerer may "*become*" and ultimately attain his true *WILL*, and the realization of his "higher self". Without Thelema, Xeper could never have been, for it is by Thelema that Xeper is possible.

The universe is not reality... It is only a dream. Consciousness alone exists. A single consciousness alone exists, isolated in a void of nothingness.

There is no God. There is no other consciousness besides that of the One. It sleeps. It dreams. As it awakens from one dream, another dream begins. There is no reality for it to awake to. There is nothing outside of consciousness. The universe seems real to the characters in the dream but what they perceive as "self" does not exist. The consciousness of the many are the consciousness of the One. The lives of the many are the dreams of the One.

ZEPAR
DEFORMS THE UNBORN

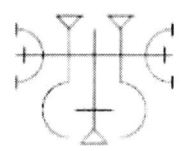

Sex Magic and Ritual

Sex magic means using your sexuality in order to work magic. This technique is not new nor outrageous; although usually kept secret many esoteric systems use sexuality for spiritual and magical aims. Examples of such traditions are witchcraft, shamanism, alchemy, Buddhism and Hinduism and ancient Egyptian religion.
A probably more known form of sex magic is the ceremonial sexual union of man and woman on the land to ensure a good crop. Their fertility act should encourage the land to deliver a rich harvest. Western sex magic has its roots in Hebrew kabala and is spread further through several occult doctrines like the knights templar and the free

masons.

Nowadays sex magic is a beautiful way of giving sex back its rightful place of sacred sexuality. It is a firm invitation to leave the trail of the sneaky, hidden-in-the-dark and 'sinful' sex most of us have grown up with. It is a call to stop fighting this most powerful human force and to make use of its possibilities.

Since sexuality is a gift from God/the Goddess it has to be divine. Within an open and respectful sexual relationship we can experience ourselves in all our aspects: the animal part, the human part and the divine flame within. Thus the beast-man-God is connected, as well as the beast-woman-Goddess.

During sexual arousal an enormous amount of energy can be channeled upwards from the genitals along the spine to the top of the head. On its way up this energy fills and cleans blockages in the chakras, caused by emotional and psychological wounds. This explains why several spiritual paths view sexual yoga as a shortcut to enlightenment.

The strong sexual force is the 'raw oil of our body' as Lama Yeshe stated. Several practitioners of sex magic reported that this form of magic turned out to be much stronger then the ceremonial magic they had practiced before.

Sex magic does not require previous knowledge of ceremonial magic. Anyone who is dedicated to controlling and directing his or her sexual energies for magical work, and who has a reasonable physical condition, is able to perform sex magic.

In sex magic we basically focus on a goal by affirmation, visualization etc.; we raise much energy through prolonged sexual arousal and we release the energy at the moment of orgasm.

The goal in sex magic can be the achievement or attraction of anything wished in the physical world, like a new house, a better relationship or a healing. It can also be the charging of magical tools or talismans. And the goal can be spiritual development.

This controlled form of love-making for higher purposes is often mentioned as the ultimate explanation of Crowley's famous statement *"Love is the Law, Love under Will."*

By love Crowley meant the uniting of the opposites masculine and feminine, active and receptive, and not so much romantic love.

Orgasm is considered to be the moment when *'the gates of heaven open up'*, for a while the barriers between the restricted physical world and the limitless heavens dissolve.

During the precious orgasmic moments we swing away our magical desire into the universe with enormous power and a *'magical child'* is born. This magical child is the astral effect of our magical action that will result in manifestation.

The sexual fluids of man and woman are charged with powerful qualities because of their magic and they can be used for several purposes.

Sex magic orgasms will be intense. And after a ritual with a partner I feel reverent and grateful, realizing that we have shared something truly meaning.

Once you know the depths and values of sex magic I wonder if a partner who would prefer to stick to *'normal'* sex could any longer satisfy your needs.

Many suggested Succubus and Incubi take semen from nocturnal emissions, or some incubi squeezed semen out of corpses. When the Devil appeared at the Sabbat, especially in the form of a Goat-Man or Black Man (Black Ash or covered in Mud) his member would be as large as a mule's, being as thick as possible, and would cause all of the presiding witches to be enflamed with lust, that each may know the devil in this way.

You may also create Succubus and Incubi to copulate with by dreams. This is done simply by creating a sigil or image which represents the form you desire. The more advanced sorcerer may invoke by some means of ritual a daemon or spirit intelligence. You visualize the sigil and then forming the body according to your carnal desire. You will then masturbate or use other means of self-stimulation, all the while focusing on the demon in question.

At the moment of ejaculation or organism anoint the sigil with the elixir. You may bind the sigil with a pouch or some way of cover, along with proper oils attributed to the daemon. You may also bury the pouch if you wish, when seeking copulation or inspiration; simply focus upon the sigil itself. You will notice dreaming sexual congress, which may awaken you aroused. To destroy the spirit, burn and cover the pouch and contents with salt.

Sinister chant is divided into three distinct

methods, all of which have the same general aim - to produce magical energy. The type and effect of this energy varies according to the method employed.

The first method is the vibration of words and phrases; the second is chanting, and the third is 'Esoteric Chant' - that is, the following of a specific text which is chanted in one of the esoteric modes.

Vibration is the simplest method, and involves the individual 'projecting' the sound. A deep breath is taken, and the first part of the word to be vibrated is 'expelled' with the exhalation of breath. This exhalation must be controlled - that is, the intensity of sound should be prolonged (not less than ten seconds for each part of the word) and as constant as possible. The person undertaking the vibration then inhales, and the process is repeated for the second part of the word and so on.

Thus 'Satanas' would be vibrated as *Sa - tan - as*. The vibration is not a shout or a scream but a concentration of sound energy. Vibration should involve the whole body and should be a physical effort.

Regular practice is essential in mastering the

technique, and the individual should learn to project at varying distances (from ten to thirty feet or more) as well as enhance the power of the vibration itself. The essence of the method is controlled sound of the same intensity throughout each part of the word and the whole word and/or text.

Chanting is essentially the singing of words or text in a regular 'monotone' - that is, in the same key, although the last part of the chant is usually 'embellished' to a certain extent by first chanting on a higher note and then a lower one. The pace of the chant varies, and can be slow (or 'funereal') or fast (or ecstatic) depending on the ceremony and the mood of the participants.

It is one of the tasks of the Master or Mistress who runs the Temple to train the congregation and new members in all three methods of chant, and to this end regular sessions of practice should be held. Chant, of whatever type, when correctly performed is one of the keys to the generation of magical energy during a ceremonial ritual and, like the dramatic performance of a ritual, its importance cannot be overemphasized.

Book of Satanic Ritual

Diabolus

Dies irae, dies illa
Solvet Saeclum in favilla
Teste Satan cum sibylla.
Quantos tremor est futurus
Quando Vindex est venturus
Cuncta stricte discussurus.
Dies irae, dies illa!

Sanctus Satanas

Sanctus Satanas, Sanctus
Dominus Diabolus Sabaoth.
Satanas - venire!
Satanas - venire!
Ave, Satanas, ave Satanas.
Tui sunt caeli,
Tua est terra,
Ave Satanas!

Oriens Splendor

Oriens splendor lucis aeternae

Book of Satanic Ritual

Et Lucifer justitae: veni
Et illumine sedentes in tenebris
Et umbra mortis.

Invocation to Baphomet

We stand armed and dangerous before the bloody fields of history;
Devoid of dogma – but ready to carve, to defy the transient:
Ready to stab forth with our penetrative will,
Strain every leash, run yelling down the mountainside of Man:
Ready and willing to immolate world upon world
With our stunning blaze.
And let them all sing that WE were here, as Masters
Among the failing speciens called Man.
Our being took form in defiance
To stand before your killing gaze.
And now we travel from flame to flame
And tower from the will to the glory!
AGIOS O BAPHOMET! AGIOS O BAPHOMET!

To you, Satan, Prince of Darkness and Lord of the

Book of Satanic Ritual

Earth, I dedicate this Temple: let it become, like my body, A vessel for your power and an expression of your glory!
With this salt I seal the power of Satan in!
With this earth I dedicate my Temple. Satanas - venire! Satanas venire! Agios O Baphomet! I am god imbued with your glory!

Book of Satanic Ritual

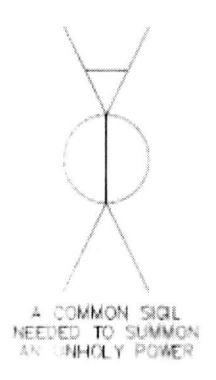

A COMMON SIGIL
NEEDED TO SUMMON
AN UNHOLY POWER

Rite of Ordination

I have given myself as a sacrifice upon the altar of Satan.
I have descended into the underworld, crossing the River Styx.
I have been baptized in the River Styx and in the Flames of Hell.
I have called upon the Lord of the Underworld, the Lord of the Dead,
And in calling upon the Lord of the Underworld,

Book of Satanic Ritual

the Lord of the Dead,
I have become the Lord of the Underworld, the Lord of the Dead.
I have sat upon the Throne of the Underworld, as Lord of the Underworld and Lord of the Dead.
I have taken the Queen of the Underworld, the Queen of the Dead, as my wife and as my lover.
But I am reborn in the Image of Satan, as a living demon in the flesh.
(dip forefinger of left hand in "unholy anointing oil", draw inverted pentagram on forehead, then say:)
I am Ordained as a priest of the Dark Lord and as an Ambassador of His Infernal Empire.

Invocation of the Lord of the Earth

I call upon the Lord of the Earth, the Horned God of the Earth.
Pan, Bacchus, Dionysus, Kernunnos, Herne,
Lord of the Earth, Horned God of the Earth,
Come forth and manifest thyself.
Lord of the Earth, I invoke thee.
Lord of the Earth, I summon thee.
Lord of the Earth, I conjure thee.

Come forth, Lord of the Earth, and manifest thyself
Within this body, this temple which I have prepared.
Come forth, Lord of the Earth, and manifest thyself.
Come forth, Lord of the Earth, and manifest thyself.

Invocation of Hecate

Hecate, I invoke thee.
Hecate, I summon thee.
Hecate, I conjure thee.
Come forth, Hecate, and manifest thyself
Within this body, this temple which I have prepared.
Come forth, Hecate, and manifest thyself.
Come forth, Hecate, and manifest thyself.
Open wide thy gate that I may cross.
Open wide thy gate that I may ascend the planetary spheres.
Come forth, Hecate, and manifest thyself.
Come forth, Hecate, and manifest thyself.
(drink from chalice, then say:) I have crossed the

Book of Satanic Ritual

Lunar Sphere.

Invocation of Thoth

Thoth, I invoke thee.
Thoth, I summon thee.
Thoth, I conjure thee.
Come forth, Thoth, and manifest thyself
Within this body, this temple which I have prepared.
Come forth, Thoth, and manifest thyself.
Come forth, Thoth, and manifest thyself.
Open wide thy gate that I may cross.
Open wide thy gate that I may ascend the planetary spheres.
Come forth, Thoth, and manifest thyself.
Come forth, Thoth, and manifest thyself.
(drink from chalice, then say:) I have crossed the Mercurial Sphere.

Invocation of Ishtar

Ishtar, I invoke thee.
Ishtar, I summon thee.

Ishtar, I conjure thee.
Come forth, Ishtar, and manifest thyself
Within this body, this temple which I have prepared.
Come forth, Ishtar, and manifest thyself.
Come forth, Ishtar, and manifest thyself.
Open wide thy gate that I may cross.
Open wide thy gate that I may ascend the planetary spheres.
Come forth, Ishtar, and manifest thyself.
Come forth, Ishtar, and manifest thyself.
(drink from chalice, then say:) I have crossed the Venuscian Sphere.

Invocation of Azael

Azael, I invoke thee.
Azael, I summon thee.
Azael, I conjure thee.
Come forth, Azael, and manifest thyself
Within this body, this temple which I have prepared.
Come forth, Azael, and manifest thyself.
Come forth, Azael, and manifest thyself.

Book of Satanic Ritual

Open wide thy gate that I may cross.
Open wide thy gate that I may ascend the planetary spheres.
Come forth, Azael, and manifest thyself.
Come forth, Azael, and manifest thyself.
(drink from chalice, then say:) I have crossed the Solar Sphere.

Invocation of Abaddon

Abaddon, I invoke thee.
Abaddon, I summon thee.
Abaddon, I conjure thee.
Come forth, Abaddon, and manifest thyself
Within this body, this temple which I have prepared.
Come forth, Abaddon, and manifest thyself.
Come forth, Abaddon, and manifest thyself.
Open wide thy gate that I may cross.
Open wide thy gate that I may ascend the planetary spheres.
Come forth, Abaddon, and manifest thyself.
Come forth, Abaddon, and manifest thyself.
(drink from chalice, then say:) I have crossed the

Martian Sphere.

Invocation of Marduk

Marduk, I invoke thee.
Marduk, I summon thee.
Marduk, I conjure thee.
Come forth, Marduk, and manifest thyself
Within this body, this temple which I have prepared.
Come forth, Marduk, and manifest thyself.
Come forth, Marduk, and manifest thyself.
Open wide thy gate that I may cross.
Open wide thy gate that I may ascend the planetary spheres.
Come forth, Marduk, and manifest thyself.
Come forth, Marduk, and manifest thyself.
(drink from chalice, then say:) I have crossed the Jupiterian Sphere.

Book of Satanic Ritual

Invocation of Cronus

Cronus, I invoke thee.
Cronus, I summon thee.
Cronus, I conjure thee.
Come forth, Cronus, and manifest thyself
Within this body, this temple which I have prepared.
Come forth, Cronus, and manifest thyself.
Come forth, Cronus, and manifest thyself.
Open wide thy gate that I may cross.
Open wide thy gate that I may ascend the planetary spheres.
Come forth, Cronus, and manifest thyself.
Come forth, Cronus, and manifest thyself.
(drink from chalice, then say:) I have crossed the Saturnian Sphere.

Invocation of Lillith

Lillith, I invoke thee.
Lillith, I summon thee.
Lillith, I conjure thee.
Come forth, Lillith, and manifest thyself

Within this body, this temple which I have prepared.
Come forth, Lillith, and manifest thyself.
Open wide thy gate that I may cross.
Open wide thy gate that I may descend to the Realm of Chaos.
Come forth, Lillith, and manifest thyself.
Come forth, Lillith, and manifest thyself.
(drink from chalice)

Book of Satanic Ritual

Book of Satanic Ritual

KALI YUGA, AN
ANCIENT SORCERY

"If power corrupts and absolute power corrupts absolutely, then the omnipotent creator of heaven and earth must be the most evil son-of-a-bitch who ever lived. Non-Christians, we are told, are damned to hell because they have not accepted Christ as their personal savior. Non-Catholics, we are told, are damned to hell because they have rejected God's Holy Church. And Catholics, we are told, are damned to hell for bowing down to and worshiping graven images. The irony of organized religious thought is the damnation of all, regardless of belief or quality of life."

                      Magus Tsirk Susej

"It is too often assumed that if a magician curses someone the victim will meet with an accident or fall ill. This is an oversimplification. Often the most profound magical workings are those which engage the assistance of other unknown human beings in order to effect the magician's will. A magician's destructive wish toward another may be justified by all laws of natural ethic and fair play, but the force that he summons may be wielded by a mean, worthless person-one whom the magician himself would despise-in order to complete the working. Oddly enough, this manner of operations can be employed for benevolent or amorous-rather than destructive-ends with equal success."

                The Satanic Rituals - Anton LaVey

There are those in Satanic Magic who practice Cognitive Magic; the use of the mind for the sake of magic ritual. Some practice this exclusively and never actually enter an inner sanctum except in their minds. There have been doubts concerning the effectiveness of this method and some actually claim greater success resulting from rituals than that of "in body" rituals. The one thing that is known for sure is the practice does exist.

The power of the mind is at the core of magic and the practice of rituals. Even the rituals performed as in a group setting is at its essence – cognitive. The thoughts of the practitioner actually drive the ritual and even the "sacrifice ritual" must use the imagination to be fully realized. Thoughts and ideas are what stimulate the Magus to open a ceremony and expect a result from a casting of a spell or hex. Without the powerful mind, we as followers of the LHP are rendered impotent.

Astral Projection has opened the way for the Satanist to use that all-powerful organ – the brain. Transverse time and slipping the bounds of gravity, the practitioner can easily create, perform and participate in the results of magic without physically leaving the comfort of their home.

As for exercising the imagination, children create a virtual reality in their minds from the age of toddler. As a child grows older, the accepted norms of life indelibly snuff out the power of the mind in exchange for being accepted by peers. No one wants to feel like an outcast at such an impressionable and critical age of development and so those things – paranormal and otherwise – are discarded from the child's psyche. From that point onward, the magic is forgotten (or ignored) and the conformance in society takes priority.

There are however, a select few who do not forget; do not abandon that which is given to us all. They may leave the path for a while or even learn to mask their talent but for those few, magic remains real and the cognitive ability remains firmly intact. In the case of a Satanist who takes this gift and fully develops it, the sky is not the limit………….there are no limits.

I know several such individuals and I must admit, their ritual results are astounding and impressive. One such acquaintance has what I call "razor-sharp" cognitive skills. She was the victim of religious and sexual abuse from a young age at the hands of a quasi-Christian cult. Her only fond memories from childhood revolve around magic and her unique gift. She is probably the most normal people in appearance; friendly almost to a fault and yet she has the ability to wage Satanic war upon those she wishes to suffer.

As with most people who challenge her ability in half belief, she delivers promptly with what she calls her "candle trick". A candle of anyone's choosing is lit in the center of a room; well beyond her reach. There is no mambo jumbo or waving hands around or any other of the parlor trick tactics. She simple stares at the flame and after a moment, the flame extinguishes.

Exactly one minute later, she makes the candle relight. For those who still doubt, she stares at the candle and again extinguishes it.

She smiles and everyone witnessing nervously laughs.

Her Satanic curses are backed up with results. Her sister's love interest cheated; 3 months later after a cognitive ritual, the love interest died of prostate cancer. Recently, her power was made manifest for a member of our coven who had been sued for child support in a bitter divorce. The petitioner was killed in a car wreck two weeks ago. Coincidence? Perhaps, save the fact that she told our group what would happen before it actually happened.

I have huge respect for these gifted ones who

Book of Satanic Ritual

continue to develop that gift. I do not have that gift but I admire those who do. Using the mind to its fullest is something all humans should strive for. For those reading this who have this wonderful gift, I am truly envious.

BTW, Her father who abused her was burned alive in a house fire............drunk and passed out. See, something good does come from bad situations..........occasionally.

Book of Satanic Ritual

TO SUMMON A MYRIAD
WHICH IS 20,736
OF HELL'S MINIONS

The Satanic Ritual

Satanas vobiscum. Palas aron ozinomas Geheamel cla orlay Baske bano tudan donas Berec he pantaras tay.

Amen . . . Evil from us deliver but . . . Temptation into not us lead and . . . Us against trespass who those forgive we as . . . Trespasses our us forgive and . . . Bread daily our day this us give . . . Heaven in is it as earth on . . . Done be will thy . . . Come kingdom thy . . . Name thy be hallowed . . . Heaven in art who . . . Father our. Eva, Ave Satanas! Vade Lilith, Deus maledictus est!! Gloria tibi! Domine Lucifere, per omnia

Book of Satanic Ritual

saecula saeculorum. Rege Satanas! In the name of Satan, ruler of Earth, the King of the world, I command the forces of darkness to bestow their infernal power upon us and open wide the gates of Hell, And come forth from the abyss to bless this unholy treatise!

It has been my desire to transmit knowledge that will afford followers of the LHP the opportunity to deepen their magical skills and understanding. I have described the result of the invocation but in this part, I wish to discuss the actual process of conjuration and the subtle, yet inestimable, concepts of Satanic Magic.

I have touched upon some of the mechanics of demonic ritual in previous posts. The actual implements, approbation, tools, techniques, etc. are outlined in the Book of Satanic Magic so I will not cover them in this book.

I will however open the reader to the acceptance and responsiveness of demonic powers that culminate into an incontrovertible corollary for the practitioner.

First, let me point out that the ways of magic are not exclusive to the Magus; anyone with the proper training, tenacity, patience and determination can expect consummate results. As with anything, the reward is equally proportionate to the investment made by the practitioner. The mind and body must be attuned to the slightest dimensional harmonics to make compensatory redress and lessen the attenuate course of action.

"As the ceremony is opened, you should pay close attention to vibrations, sounds, temperature changes, etc. Some demons manifest as slight changes in ambient lighting produced by candlelight. Others will bring an uneasy "chill" to the otherwise temperate conditions of the sanctum. I have experienced the movement of small objects caused by a quick puff of air from an undetermined direction. These are all examples however, none are constantly present. Demons are individuals (as we) and they make their entrance as they wish."

The choice of demonic force desired is usually according to the ritual being conducted; In Rem: Destruction ritual would necessitate a menacing and contentious being with the ability to do your evil dealing without any reservation whatsoever.

I prefer a demon such as Samael (Demon of Death) for this type of working. The match of tactic and tactician is very important. This is magic where real and tangible results are produced; magic is not a stratagem.

The Ritual of Baphomet can be used as an opening for the Ritual of Black Flame. Both rituals are precursors to a summons and both work well together. Advantageous transitions into the conjurations can be found by using these rituals. The right frame of mind is both necessary and conspicuous for the practitioner. One only has to experience the true working of the conjure to be forever transformed through a Satanic metamorphosis; just as caterpillar to chrysalis (pupa) to the butterfly. All actions play out to the five senses and some are overwhelming. For example, when the being Azazel (that great shepherd and scapegoat) materializes, there is always a sound that reminds me of a goat bleating. As I mentioned in the earlier posts, each being is as individual as we humans.

The ringing of a bell nine (9) times (during ritual work) clears the air inside the Inner Sanctum. Anton Lavey described the Inner Sanctum as the "intellectual decompression chamber" in his book The Satanic Bible.

Clearing the air inside this "chamber" allows the resonate harmonics and low-frequency oscillation to manifest in useful Satanic vibrations. His explanation is quite simple yet cognitively advanced.

"The formalized beginning and end of the ceremony acts as a dogmatic, anti-intellectual device, the purpose of which is to disassociate the activities and frame of reference of the outside world from that of the ritual chamber, where the whole will must be employed. This facet of the ceremony is most important to the intellectual, as he especially requires the "decompression chamber" effect of the chants, bells, candles, and other trappings, before he can put his pure and willful desires to work for himself, in the projection and utilization of his imagery."

The imagery conceived in the mind plays a part and as I have discussed before, imagining the outcome of a ritual (in this case the materialization of a demon) is very important. You (and the coven) must be prepared for the visualization of the demon and the group should discuss the imagery before entering the Inner Sanctum and opening the ritual. Without this all-

Book of Satanic Ritual

important step, the members of the coven are each imagining a different outcome from the process than the other coven members; and thus confusion and a failed conjure. Speak with one voice and think as one mind within your coven and ensure everyone is mentally prepared.

Purification of the body, just as the air, is very important as well. Bathing before rituals is not only a courtesy for your coven members (who may perform fellatio on you later) but is ultimately respectful to Satan and the demons you invite into your rituals. Respect is not only desired but it is required of the hellish hosts. Any less that absolute reverence, tribute and worship is unpardonable and should never be condoned or allowed to manifest within the working coven. Members should understand and comply with this simple precept.

"There is no difference between "White" and "Black" magic, except in the smug hypocrisy, guilt-ridden righteousness and self-deceit of the "White" magician himself."
Anton Szandor Lavey

Book of Satanic Ritual

When performing any incantation, the culmination and focus of energy is vital and conjuration is no different. The focus of the group's energy allows for the frenetic controlled chaos to be channeled into a powerful medium with fantastic results. The group begins building this energy long before entering the Inner Sanctum.

This energy is identical to that of a child who is looking forward to a special event (such as the arrival of Santa Claus) and the anticipation amplifies as time passes. The magic of the coven is no different from this crude analogy. By the time the practitioner finally enters the Inner Sanctum, he/she can hardly contain them self. Thus, the unabated pure power.

I also equate this feeling to being sexually stimulated but not to the point of orgasm. The result is the same.

Book of Satanic Ritual

Book of Satanic Ritual

Dear Searcher,

If you are interested in further advancement for yourself in the Black Arts, feel free to contact me. I have counseled hundreds of those wishing to find a *solid footing* in Satanism. Everyone needs a helping hand to achieve their goals and asking for help is not a "*weakness*"; it demonstrates intelligence and a sincere intention to take the Satanic Arts seriously.

May the blessings of Hell pour upon you and provide you with your desires. I would like to hear from you.

Write me at *aleisternacht@rocketmail.com* or visit my website at *www.AleisterNacht.com*.

A~N

CPSIA information can be obtained at www.ICGtesting.com
Printed in the USA
LVOW10s2119270616

494292LV00029B/1216/P